Shekarry Old

Wrinkles; or, Hints to Sportsmen and Travellers

On Dress, Equipment, and Camp Life

Shekarry Old

Wrinkles; or, Hints to Sportsmen and Travellers
On Dress, Equipment, and Camp Life

ISBN/EAN: 9783337204891

Printed in Europe, USA, Canada, Australia, Japan

Cover: Foto ©Andreas Hilbeck / pixelio.de

More available books at **www.hansebooks.com**

WRINKLES;

OR,

HINT'S TO SPORTSMEN AND TRAVELLERS

ON

𝕯ress, 𝕰quipment, and 𝕮amp 𝕷ife.

BY

THE OLD SHEKARRY,

AUTHOR OF "THE FOREST AND THE FIELD," ETC.

A NEW EDITION, FULLY ILLUSTRATED.

𝕷ondon:

CHATTO AND WINDUS, PUBLISHERS.

1874.

LONDON:
SAVILL, EDWARDS AND CO., PRINTERS, CHANDOS STREET,
COVENT GARDEN.

INTRODUCTION.

HAVING been often applied to for information concerning the most suitable Dress, the most efficient Arms, and the best equipment for a Sportsman, I have endeavoured, in the following pages, to concentrate my ideas on these points for the benefit of the uninitiated. I have also added a description of the different modes of hunting the fiercer denizens of the Forest, and sundry practical hints upon travelling and campaigning, that may be useful to those who have not yet acquired that experience of camp-life, without which, in a wild and almost unknown country, peopled by treacherous tribes, the Traveller will have much difficulty in keeping his health sound and his skin whole.

CONTENTS.

"WRINKLES"

OR

HINTS TO SPORTSMEN AND TRAVELLERS.

CHAPTER I.

DRESS.

A Traveller's Comfort—Dress: Underclothes, Socks, Coat, Waistcoat, Trousers, and Breeches—On the Most Suitable Colour
for a Sportsman's Dress—Table of the Effect of Colour—
Braces—Boots—" The Old Shekarry's Campaigning Boot "—
Waterproof Clothes—The Old Shekarry's Poncho, or "Multum
in Parvo " Cloak: a Ground Sheet, a Cloak, a Tent, a Bed,
and a Raft—Waterproof Hunting Gear—Sou'wester, Jacket,
and Overalls—Head Gear—Leech-gaiters and Tree-leeches—
Outfit of a Sportsman for a Cruise of Six Months.

MUCH of a traveller's comfort depends upon his
dress being suitable to the climate he is in, and I
shall commence with a few hints as to the selection
of an outfit.

Shirts. All experienced travellers seem to
agree in one point, viz., the importance of wearing flannel next the skin; and no one
who has any regard for his health will neglect

B

the precaution of providing himself with shirts or under-clothing of this material, if he is at all likely to be exposed to sudden changes of climate, as it absorbs perspiration and prevents sudden chills.

In tropical climates, calico shirts may be worn, but, without flannel under-clothing, linen should never be placed next the skin.

Flannel ought to be thoroughly shrunk before making up.

Socks.   The most comfortable hose to wear are thick, but not coarse, woollen socks; but care must be taken that the tops are sufficiently elastic to prevent their slipping down, as when walking it is a great nuisance to have to stop every few minutes, to pull up your socks. They ought to fit well, particularly about the heel, so as to prevent galling or blisters.

Messrs. Thresher and Glenny, in the Strand, have been long celebrated for their socks, shirts, and under-clothing.

The material for a traveller's dress entirely depends upon the climate he is going to.

For a temperate climate, woollen tweed, or angolas are, perhaps, the best general wear; but for the tropics, I prefer coloured flannel, as being more comfortable and easier to wash.

For a sportsman, well dressed deer-skin is the best material; when that is not procurable, mole-skin, velveteen, corderoy, fustian, canvas, duck, or karkee (coloured cotton), may be used.

A traveller ought to study *comfort* more than elegance, in the cut of his clothes, and little attention should be paid to change of fashion.

Sanguinetti, of Regent Street, in former days, used to be a famous tailor of "clothes for the bush," but I think he has gone the way of all flesh, as his establishment has vanished, and his mantle appears to have descended upon Bird, of 13, Waterloo Place, a practical man, who knows how to cut out "hunting togs," so as to be comfortable in any position, without being baggy,

which is a great desideratum when forcing one's
way through dense forest.

My own experience leads me to believe that a
short blouse-shaped tunic, with sleeves and wrist-
bands, like a shirt, straight collar, and plenty of
well-cut pockets, is most comfortable for general
wear. Mr. Bird has built me a shooting-coat, with
waterproof arrangements for carrying two dozen
cartridges, just below the waist, which appears to
me to be everything that can be desired.

Waistcoats ought to be cut long, with four
pockets, and the substance behind ought to be as
thick and warm as the material of which the
waistcoat is made.

Some sportsmen prefer having a waistcoat
made with sleeves like a jacket, and in that case
there are no sleeves to the coat, simply armholes.
In shooting upon the moors, sometimes this is a
useful dodge, as during the heat of the day the
outer garment can be dispensed with, and carried
by a beater. When worn, this rather peculiar
arrangement cannot be distinguished.

Mr. Cooper, a sportsman of Yorkshire celebrity, was the first to show me this arrangement.

For shooting, I prefer breeches, cut so as to come well below the calf, and tying with flat tape over the sock, an arrangement that does away with the necessity of long stockings and garters [which are only suitable to women] when wearing boots or gaiters. There should be no hem at the bottom of the legs of the breeches, or it may form a ridge, and gall the legs.

For riding, nothing is so comfortable as leather breeches, but thick moleskin, doubled inside the legs, is not bad wear.

In Equatorial Africa, during the intense heat of the day, I generally wore a kilt and flannel shirt, boots and gaiters, which dress I found cooler and less liable to gall than trousers. Many good sportsmen prefer the kilt to any other dress, on account of the freedom and play it allows the limbs.

Colour.

The sportsman should have all his dress as nearly as possible of the same colour as the general aspect of the country he is going to shoot over.

Thus, when he is deer-stalking, or tracking large game in woods before the leaf has fallen, green is the best colour; when the trees are bare, dark brown—the colour of the trunk and branches. Is he after antelope on the plain, or ibex amongst the rocks, drab is the best colour. Should he be waging war against the grisly bear, or hunting chamois bouquetin in the snow, he would be able to get much nearer to his game if all his clothes were white.

Even in ordinary small game shooting, the sportsman will stand a much better chance of making, if he attends to this plan of dressing.

The following tables were constructed with great care from a series of experiments I made with targets of different coloured cloth, under various circumstances and at different distances, in order to assist volunteer corps in the selection of the most suitable colour for their uniform.

The figure 1 denotes the most visible; 7 the least so; 0 invisible.

Colours.	At Three Hundred Yards.								At Six Hundred Yards.								One Mile.
	Open Country.	Wooded Country.	Rocky Ground.	Sea Shore.	Over Water.	Against Sky.	Against Earthworks.	Against Stone Fortifications.	Open Country.	Wooded Country.	Rocky Ground.	Sea Shore.	Over Water.	Against Sky.	Against Earthworks.	Against Stone Fortifications.	
Scarlet	4	3	4	3	2	4	5	4	4	2	5	3	2	3	5	4	5
Green (Rifle)	3	6	5	4	4	2	4	3	3	7	4	5	4	4	4	3	3
Blue (Royal)	2	4	4	3	5	3	3	2	2	6	3	4	5	4	3	2	2
White	1	1	1	2	1	4	1	2	1	1	1	1	1	5	1	2	1
Gray	7	6	7	7	7	6	6	7	6	7	0	7	0	7	0	7	6
Brown (dead leaf)	7	7	7	6	6	5	5	7	7	0	0	6	0	6	0	6	7

Colours.	At Three Hundred Yards distant.											
	On a Clear Day.				On a Cloudy Day.						Bright Moonlight.	Starlight.
	Daybreak.	Sunrise.	Mid-day.	Sunset.	Daybreak.	Sunrise.	Mid-day.	Sunset.	Rain.	Rain and Fog.		
Scarlet	4	3	3	4	4	3	4	6	3	3	4	5
Green (Rifle)	3	4	4	3	7	7	3	0	4	4	3	4
Blue (Royal)	2	5	3	2	6	6	3	0	4	4	3	4
White	1	1	1	1	1	1	1	5	0	1	1	1
Gray	7	6	7	5	0	0	0	0	2	6	0	0
Brown (dead leaf)	6	7	6	6	0	0	6	0	6	7	7	7

By these Tables it will be seen, that gray or brown are colours that are less distinguishable than any other; they are, consequently, the most suitable for the dress of sportsmen.

Braces. I think braces are a convenience, and always use them when wearing thick clothing; but as many sportsmen dispense with them altogether, perhaps use is second nature. However, having the waist compressed by tight trouser-bands is not my idea of comfort. A woman's hips are made to hang petticoats on, but a man is differently formed in that respect, and his garments will only keep up by compression.

Boots. A traveller's comfort and a sportsman's efficiency depends more on his boots than upon any other portion of his dress, and great attention ought to be paid to their fitting the foot well, and having a sufficiently broad tread.

For many years I wore ankle-boots and gaiters, and provided the former fit, and the latter are well cut, so as to prevent extraneous matter from getting in, they are comfortable wear.

After a time, however, I began to think that lacing-up boots and buttoning gaiters was unnecessary trouble (besides, not one man in a dozen can cut a gaiter to fit properly), so I devised a campaigning boot upon a plan of my own, which experience has proved to be a more comfortable and serviceable article. I herewith give a sketch of my invention, which Stokes, a *ci-devant* trooper, of Coventry Street and Aldershot, has carried out very efficiently.

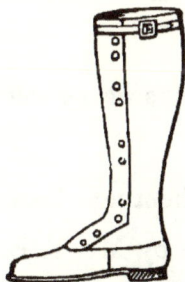

The Old Shekarry's Campaigning Boot.

The best material for making this boot is of deer-skin, doubled over the foot when it is procurable, but brown or drab waterproof canvas is not a bad substitute, being footed with leather. It ought to fit the leg well, and the leather uppers should be cut so as to compress the foot as little as possible.

A shooting-boot ought to be waterproof to be thoroughly comfortable, and the real article is as unlike as possible those ponderous pieces of machinery one sees in shop-windows ticketed "for the moors." They must be of first-class material to be serviceable, but light, so as not to fatigue the wearer; and they should also fit well, so as not to gall, cause blisters, and make the feet sore. A *well-fitting* boot is as necessary to a sportsman as a true shooting rifle.

For stalking large game, boots should be made with single leather flexible soles, so as to prevent the footstep being heard.

It is a great mistake to think that a *heavy* sole is necessary for a shooting-boot.

A very excellent waterpoof shooting boot, called " *The Idstone Boot*," is made by Mr. T. E. Cording, 231, Strand, of a material that requires no dressing, and still always keeps soft and pliable.

Waterproof Clothes. The traveller and sportsman should ever be prepared for any sudden change of climate, and always have warm clothing at hand, as very often whilst the days are intensely hot the nights are chilly, and the temperature varies according to the elevation attained. It is of the greatest importance that his outer covering should be of a texture sufficiently close to prevent the wind blowing through it, or thickness is of little avail in keeping out intense cold; hence the great advantage of buffalo robes and mackintosh garments.

For general use, Cording's waterproof material far surpasses all other, as it is guaranteed to stand any climate, and rolls up in a small compass.

Every traveller ought to provide himself with a cloak or coat and sou'wester of this material, which should be always kept handy and ready for use, more especially in night travelling, for nothing tries a man's constitution more than exposure to night-dews after the exhaustion and lassitude caused by an intensely hot day. Rheumatism and fever are anything but agreeable companions, as I have often found to my cost; and a little timely precaution may avert serious consequences.

Having had much "roughing it" in my time, often with very small means and few conveniences, I have been compelled to study how to make one article serve in a variety of ways. When baggage is obliged to be limited and carriage is difficult to obtain, it is very desirable to have *multum in parco*.

I shall now describe "a poncho" of my own invention, carried out by Mr. Cording, of 231, Strand, which serves as a ground-sheet, a tent, a bed covering, or even, if required, a boat or raft for crossing rivers.

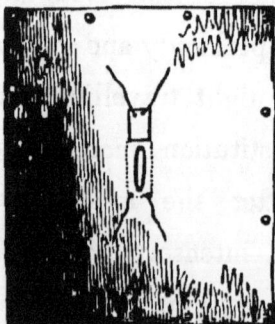

The Ground-Sheet.

It consists of waterproof canvas, 8 feet by 7 feet 6 inches in size, with a longitudinal slit in the centre, and eylet-holes worked all round, as in the cut, when it serves as a ground-sheet and coverlet.

It forms a comfortable cloak for riding or walking, by putting it on and slipping the head through the hole in the centre, the corners buttoning up in the inside if in the way.

In travelling through mangrove swamps on the West Coast of Equatorial Africa, where there was no solid ground on which

The Cloak.

to pitch a tent, I used to sleep in a hammock slung between trees, and whilst following up the spoor of a herd of elephant, or when surrounded by hostile tribes, and I dare not clear a few yards of bush in the forest lest the sounds of the axe should be heard and give the alarm, my poncho, rigged up like a pent roof, in this fashion, afforded me a shelter impervious to the weather.

The Bivouac.

For a boat or raft, the poncho should be constructed with an oval ring, two feet wide all
round, which can be inflated with air. A wooden
or basket-work bottom (anywhere easily constructed) is then fixed underneath, by cords
passing through the eyelet-holes, and a commodious raft, capable of containing two people, is at
once constructed, and easily worked by paddles.
By having the basket-work or wooden bottom
some inches larger than the inflated poncho, all
danger of the cylinder being pierced by snags of
rocks, or branches, is avoided.

Mr. Cording has my pattern poncho, and fully
understands its manufacture.

The "Old Shekarry's" Poncho Raft.

The Sou'wester.

The Jacket.

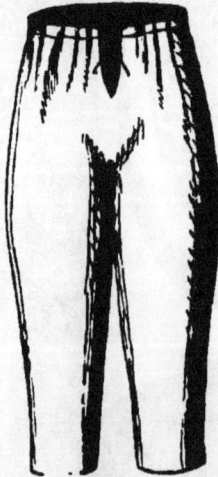

The Overalls.

For shooting in the wet season, I have a complete waterproof suit, which I find much more handy when making my way after large game, through thick bush.

The cuts will explain my style of rig, which is comfortable, if not elegant. Care must, however, be taken that they are made of a material that will stand a tropical climate; as a very nice-looking suit I bought from Box, of Charing Cross, proved utterly useless on the West Coast of Africa, as,

the first time I had occasion to use it, I found
it so stuck together, that it was torn into shreds
before I could open it out.

Head-Gear.   The best covering for the head in
tropical climates is pith " *solar topee*,"
or helmet, such as old Sir Charles Napier and
Sir Colin Campbell used to wear ; or when that
is not obtainable, an Elwood's ventilating air-
chamber hat, covered with white calico, is a good
substitute. Christy, of Gracechurch Street, also
manufactures a capital hat for withstanding the
rays of the sun, which my experience leads me to
believe is almost perfect.

A leather hunting-cap,
with peaks before and
behind, is the best protection to the head for large
game-shooting in dense
forests. The front peak preserves the eyes from
glare and the face from thorns, and the one behind prevents anything from falling down the
back of the neck. I had a movable white linen

c

cover fitted to mine, as a protection from the rays of the sun during the heat of the day.

Leech Gaiters.   In forests where the tree-leech abounds, leech-gaiters must be worn, for these animals insinuate themselves into every aperture of your dress, generally making for your ankles or the back of your neck, as if by instinct.

When in such jungles it is absolutely necessary to wear leech gaiters, or long, closely-woven cotton stockings, over your socks, under your boots and gaiters, and over your breeches, as far as they will go. Even with this safeguard I have sometimes found my boots and stockings drenched with blood in the evening, though I could not ascertain how they got in.

These pests of the jungle are very insignificant in size, not being above an inch in length, or thicker than a knitting-needle; but when distended with blood they attain double that length, and are about as thick as a good-sized quill. They have the power of planting one extremity on the ground, and poising themselves erect to watch for prey, towards which they advance rapidly by doubling up the body and holding on with their head and tail. They are of a yellowish-brown colour, streaked with black, with one greenish line along the whole length of the back, and a yellow one on each side. Their bites scarcely give any pain at the time, the punctures being so small as hardly to be perceptible, but they cause an uncomfortable irritation; and with persons in a bad state of body often occasion nasty ulcers, which are slow to heal. The natives were accustomed to smear their naked legs with some peculiar kind of grease mixed with ashes, the scent of which prevented the leeches from biting, otherwise they would have been seriously inconvenienced by their attacks.

Every traveller and sportsman has his own idea and style of dress. "*As many men, so many fashions*"—but, for the benefit of the uninitiated, I will give a list of such clothes, as I consider

c 2

necessary for myself for a cruise of six months in
the bush :

8 flannel shirts (made large).
12 pairs of woollen socks.
6 pairs of brown holland or China silk pajamas.
12 pocket handkerchiefs (linen).
1 leather suit, complete (coat, breeches and waistcoat).
1 moleskin suit, complete (coat, breeches and waistcoat).
2 pairs of trousers (either moleskin, fustian or velveteen).
2 pairs of braces.
2 pairs of long cotton stockings, for leech-gaiters.
1 leather hunting cap and linen cover.
1 pith "solar topee," or air-chamber hat (for tropics).
1 soft felt wide-awake.
2 pairs of ankle boots.
2 pairs of gaiter boots.
1 Cording's waterproof suit, complete, or poncho.
1 canvas hold-all : containing comb, tooth-brush, soap, needles,
    thread, buttons, scissors, thimble, &c.
3 towels (good size).
3 napkins.

CHAPTER II.

THE EQUIPMENT OF A TRAVELLER AND A SPORTSMAN.

Oliver Cromwell's Letter upon a Soldier's Equipment—The Saddle and its Appurtenances, Bridle, Horse-gear—The Old Shekarry's "Pack Saddle"—Spurs—The Hunting Belt and its Appurtenances—The Bill-hook and Tomahawk—The Nugger Hunt Spear—The Deccan Hunt Spear—Bear Spears—The Indian Hunting Cart and its Appurtenances—The Medicine Chest and its Contents—Pocket Filters—The Old Shekarry's Pump and Filter combined — Cording's Inflatable India-Rubber Boat.

"Wisbeach, this day 11th Novr. 1642.

"Dear Friend,

"Let the saddler see to the horse-gear. I learn from one, many are ill served, and if a man has not got good weapons, horse and harness, he is naught.

"From your friend,

"OLIVER CROMWELL.

"To Auditor Squire."

Oliver Cromwell, the most practical soldier and statesman of his day, thus wrote upwards of two centuries ago; and I quote his characteristic letter, as I never read so much good advice in as few words. The first point for consideration is the horse-gear.

The Saddle.   I shall commence with "the saddle," which, to be thoroughly strong

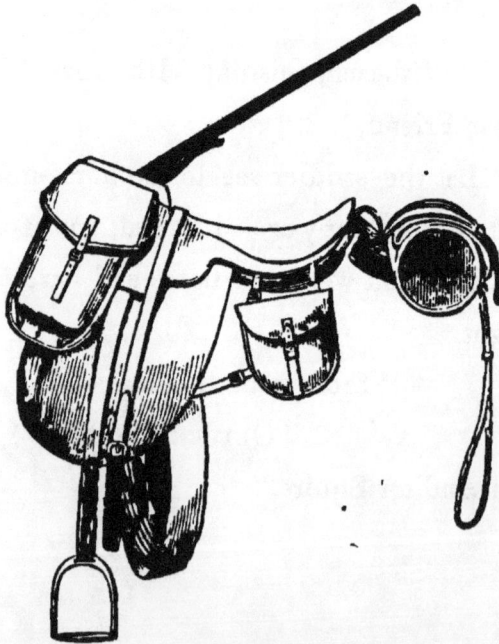

The Saddle.

and serviceable, with its appurtenances, will not weigh less than fifteen pounds. I prefer a broad, roomy, and low seat, so that I sit close to the horse, and I like it cut almost flush.

On the near side of the pommel, fastened by strong *D's*, I carry a waterproof wallet for my pistol and ammunition, which should set close and stand well forward, so as not to be in the way of the leg.

On the off-side I have a strong painted canvas bag, which is prevented from shifting forward by a leather strap that passes round the saddle-girth. Into this my gun-stock fits, the barrel passing between the right arm and the side, so that it is always handy, never in the way, and my hands are free. This method, which I learned from the Boers of Southern Africa, is perfectly safe, and by far the most convenient and the least fatiguing mode of carrying a gun I have yet seen.

On the near side of the saddle, fastened by strong *D's*, is slung my water-skin, which will

hold two gallons of water; and on the off-side a
haversack, with corn for my nag, and comestibles
for myself.

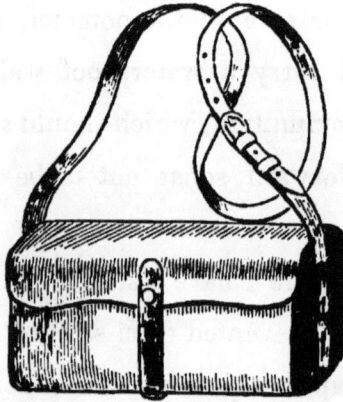

Small Valise.

Behind the crupper I carry a pad, on which
rests a very small valise (containing two pairs of
socks, flannel shirt and trousers, soap, towel, and
tooth brush—*vide* Plate, above), a ground-sheet,
macintosh cloak, and horse-cloth, which are confined in a network bag (*vide* Plate, page 25) to
prevent any article being lost *en route*. This bag

also serves for collecting forage, or carrying game, etc., on occasions.

Net-Work Bag, &c.

A couple of thin strips of felt or "numna" is useful to place under the saddle when it does not fit the horse's back, but for hard riding nothing is like a piece of oil silk laid directly under a well-stuffed saddle.

Horse's Head-Gear.

I always travel with a plain head-stall bridle (*vide* Plate, above) which has only four buckles,

two on the head-collar, one on the bit head
stall, and one on the bridoon head-stall. The
head-stall fastens to the collar by strap and
button.

The bit, bridoon and head-stall are provided
with hooks and links, by which the bits can be
slipped out of the horse's mouth for the purpose
of feeding, without taking the bridle off the
horse's head. I generally ride with a single
"Chifney bit."

Shipley, of 181, Regent Street, the most practical saddler I know, is well up in all the arrangements concerning horse-gear, and he has
been put up to all kinds of "useful dodges"
and expedients by different well-known sportsmen whom he has fitted up.

A traveller should take hobbles and knee-
halters with him to tether his horses, so that they
can graze during the night.

As a protection against thieves, steel hobbles,
made somewhat like hand-cuffs, connected by a
chain, are useful.

A comfortable English saddle, and well-fitting horse-gear, is absolutely necessary to a traveller and sportsman; and the utmost care should be taken that the former is well stuffed, so as not to gall the horse's back, as a quarter of an hour's hard riding on a badly fitting saddle may break the skin, and give a horse a sore back that will take several days to heal.

The Pack-Saddle.   There are no articles in a traveller's equipment to which more attention ought to be paid than to the pack-saddles for baggage-animals. If they do not fit the horse, mule, or bullock properly, a single day's march will, in all probability, render the animal unserviceable.

As no pack-saddle I have seen in any army seemed thoroughly to answer its purpose under all situations, I set to work and devised one after my own fashion, which I consider has many

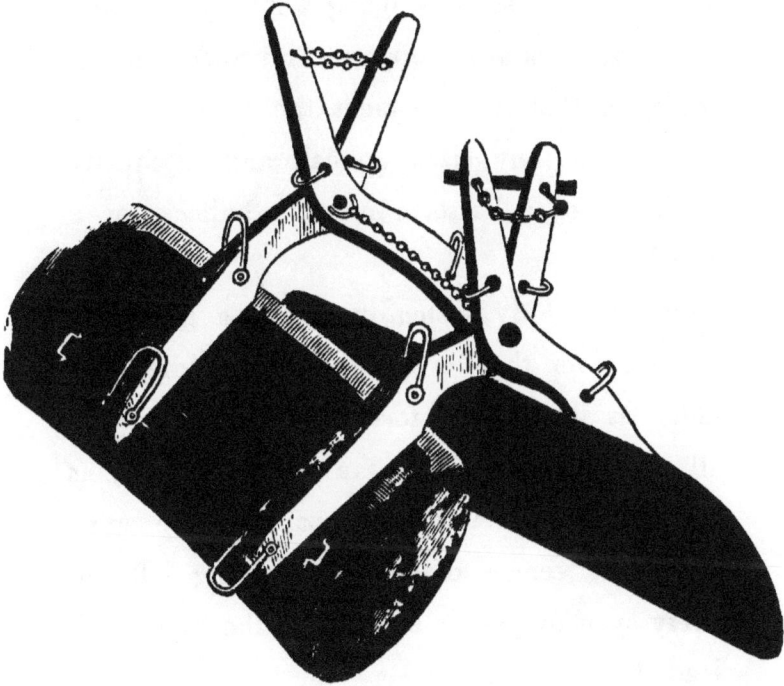

"The Old Shekarry's Pack-Saddle."

great advantages over all other systems yet adopted.

First.—The chief improvement in " The Old Shekarry's Pack-Saddle" consists in the tree, which widens or contracts by working on a pivot like a pair of scissors, being kept open at any angle by a rack at the opposite and corresponding angle, so that in a moment the saddle can be made to fit any sized animal, and is equally available for a horse, a mule, a bullock, or a camel.

Secondly.—My system possesses a great advantage over the Government pack-saddle, inasmuch as its peculiar formation does away with all possibility of *galling* an animal's back, as no weight rests upon any part of the spine itself, the centre of the back being left entirely open to the air even when the baggage is loaded.

Thirdly.—The tree, which is either entirely made of wrought iron, or of wood well strengthened with iron, closes up, and the saddle can be packed into half the space required by the system at present adopted by Government.

Fourthly.—Any tree or part of a tree will fit

any saddle, and should any part of a tree get broken, it can be replaced in two minutes, and the saddle is again serviceable, whereas in other systems, when a tree is broken, the saddle is useless.

Fifthly.—A cannon can be carried by this system of pack-saddle *over the centre* of the mule's back, *along which the weight is thus equally divided.*

In the pack-saddles adopted by Government for carrying the mountain train in Abyssinia, the gun is carried transversely—at right angles with the mule's back, or across instead of along it. The consequence of this arrangement is, that the whole weight of the gun rests upon only a small portion of the spine, instead of being evenly divided, as in the approved system, along the whole length of the animal's back, and should a stumble occur, a sprain of the spine is very likely to be the result.

Sixthly.—When baggage animals are driven

together in any number, it is almost impossible to prevent them from knocking against each other, and displacing their loads; it is therefore highly advantageous that the baggage should be carried as compactly as it can be stowed, and take up as little lateral room as possible.

In mountainous districts, where the paths are narrow, and run by the edge of precipices, this is an absolute necessity.

This saddle is amply supplied with rengs and *D's*, fixed securely on to the iron trees, so that the baggage is easily loaded, and kept securely in its place.

Seventhly.—The cost of my system of pack-saddle is about half of the price that Government lately paid for cumbrous and much less serviceable articles.

Spurs.   The best-shaped spurs for a traveller or sportsman are strong steel or brass swan-necked hunting spurs, with the rowels sufficiently raised to prevent their grating against stones or uneven ground when dismounted.

A man with long legs requires spurs with long necks, so that he may readily reach his horse's flank with the rowel; but a man with short legs, on the contrary, should have spurs with short necks, as his heels, when mounted, are close to the body of the horse.

The Hunting Belt. The Plate, page 34, is a sketch of the BELT and APPURTENANCES I usually wore when in the pursuit of large game, manufactured by Thornhill of 144, New Bond Street, the most practical man in the trade.

"THE BELT" A A is about two inches in width, and made of strong brown leather. Great attention should be paid to the sewing on of the buckles, which ought to be of forged iron.

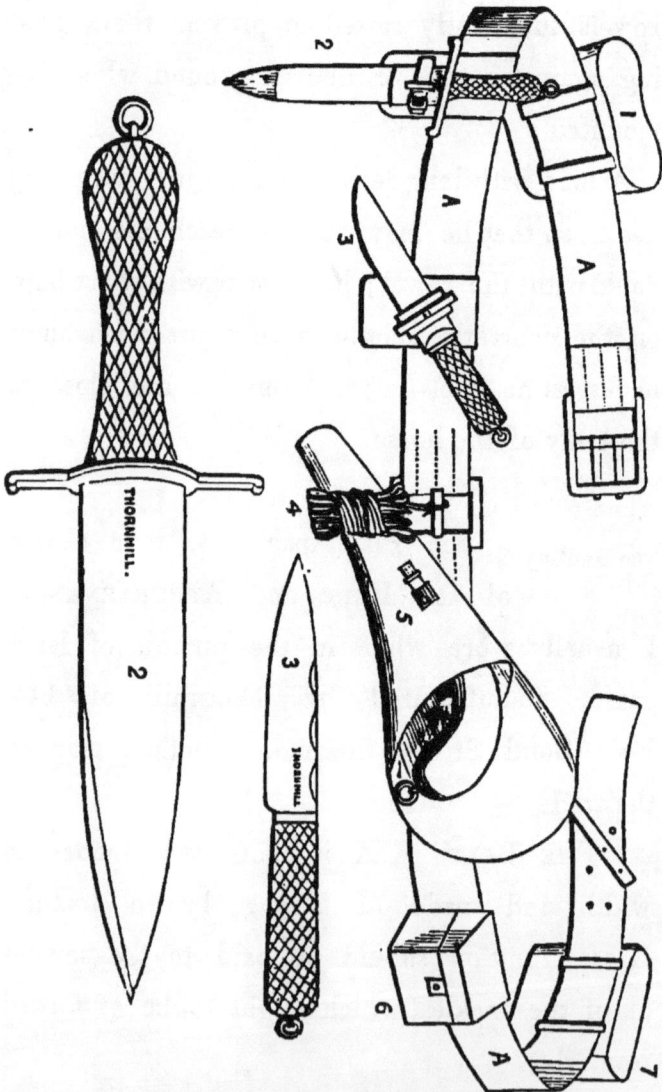

The Hunting Belt and its Appurtenances.

Fig. 1. A stout leather case containing my field-glass.

Fig. 2. My "HUNTING KNIFE." I prefer this shape to any other, as it is well suited for all purposes. In selecting a knife, great care should be taken that the point and axis of both blade and handle should be in a straight line, or a fair blow cannot be struck with effect, the weapon being liable to glance off.

With one of Thornhill's knives I can cut through a dollar; and it is absolutely necessary that the blade should be made of the best steel, for, besides its use as a weapon, it must often serve to cut branches, and even in digging for water.

Fig. 3. The "SKINNING KNIFE," made after the pattern of A. Graham, Esq., which I do not think can be improved upon.

Fig. 4. "A LINE" of strong silk, substantially fastened to a forged iron bar. This is of great use as a safeguard, in case of having to descend any steep slope or narrow ledge of rock when in the pursuit of game. It is also very useful for drawing water from wells or chasms in the rocks, tying up the arms of a prisoner, or tethering animals.

Fig. 5. "A LEATHER POUCH," containing either a double-barrel pistol or revolver [elsewhere described].

Fig. 6. "A SMALL CASE," containing matches, flint, steel, and amadou, for obtaining fire, and in a similar one the pocket filter ought to be carried.

Fig. 7. "A LEATHER POUCH," containing eight cartridges for gun or rifle, and six for the pistol.

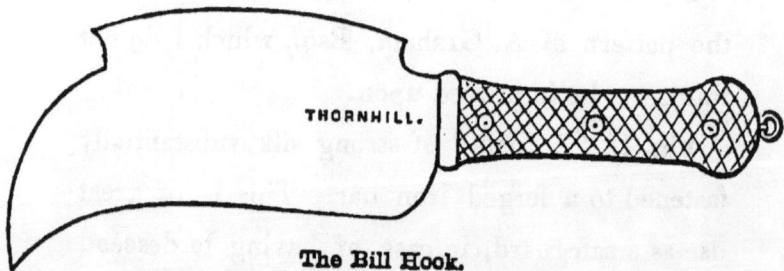

THORNHILL.

The Bill Hook.

The Bill-Hook.

Besides these articles, in some cases, when in thick jungle, it is advisable to carry a *bill-hook* for cutting a path or making a clearing. This fits in a leather case, which is easily fastened on the belt when required.

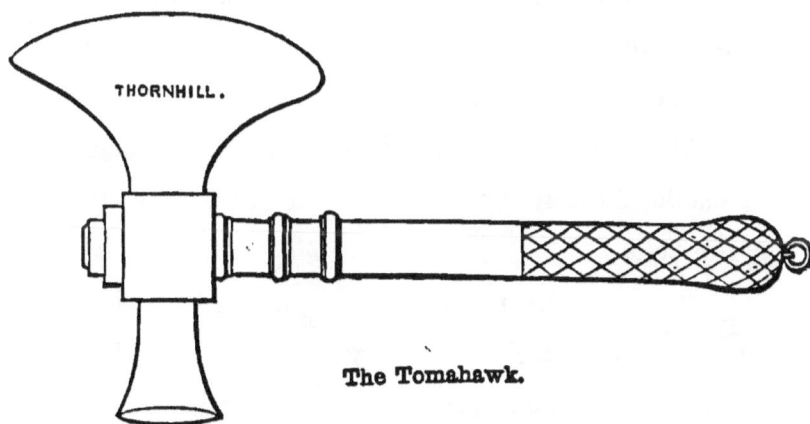

THORNHILL.

The Tomahawk.

" THE TOMAHAWK," or small axe, herewith represented, is useful in making tent-pegs, cutting up animals, and for a variety of purposes in camp life.

Last, but by no means least in importance, comes the knife, of which an engraving is given on the opposite page, and which, in addition to the ordinary blades, contains a powerful screwdriver, a saw about eight inches in length, pricker, corkscrew, hoof-picker, tweezers and lancet in one, a pair of scissors of the full length of the knife, and a couple of stout steel screws, with nuts, for mending a broken stirrup leather or any similar fracture.

All implements have rings attached, so as to enable them to be fastened with small cords to the belts.

Spears.

Every sportsman ought to provide himself with a few spear-heads, which can at any time be affixed to a bamboo with " *shellac cement.*" The best shapes for boar-spears are those called after the celebrated Indian Pig-sticking Clubs, "The Nugger" and "The Deccan" Hunts.

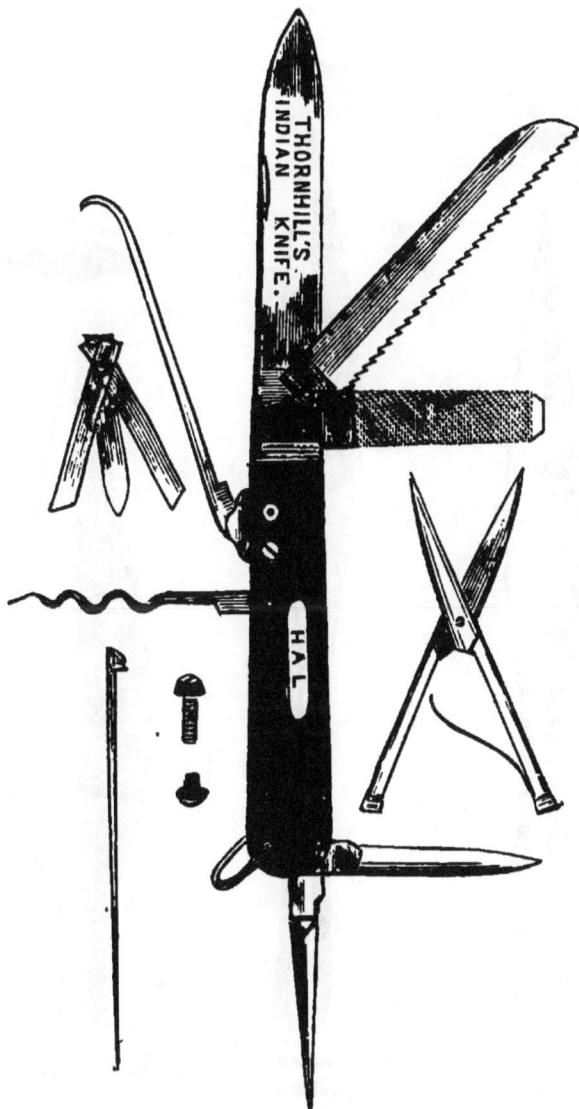

Thornhill's Indian Knife.

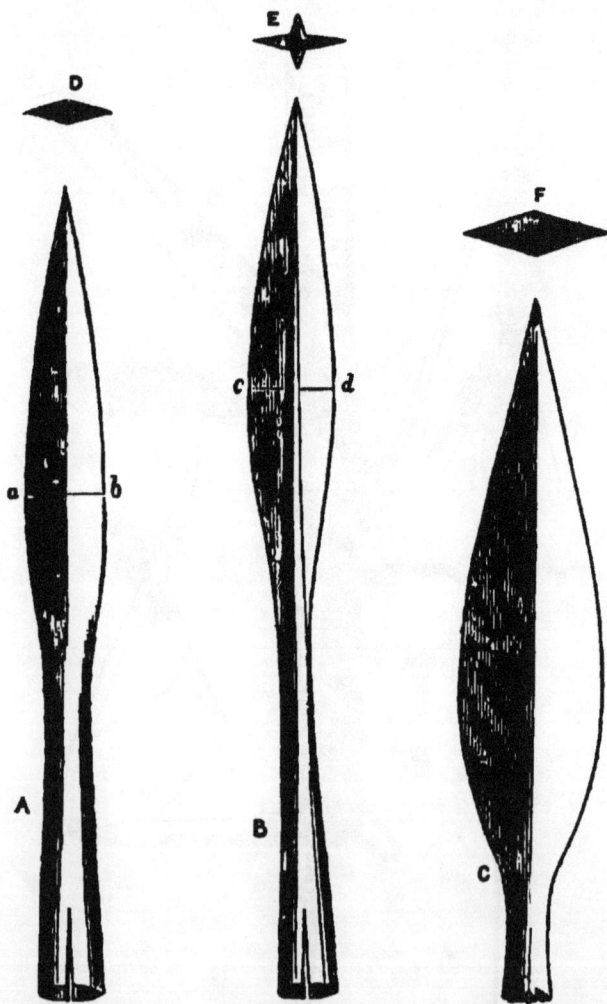

The "Nugger Hunt"   The "Deccan Hunt"   The Bear Spear.
Pattern.   Pattern.

In the foregoing Plate Fig. *A* shows the Nugger
Hunt pattern, which I consider the *ne plus ultra* of
boar-spears, the curves being gradual from point
to shank, so that it penetrates easily, and is withdrawn without difficulty. Another great advantage of this shape is, that the edge can be easily
ground, and afterwards sharpened on a hone.
(Fig D shows the section at *a b*.)

Fig. *B* is the Deccan Hunt spear pattern, also
a good spear, and preferred by some sportsmen
to that of the Nugger Hunt, because the orifice
of the wound it makes is somewhat larger, and
allows the blood to flow more freely. It is, however, more difficult to sharpen. (Fig. E shows
the section at *c d*.)

Fig. *C* is a bear-spear, somewhat similar in
shape to the Nugger Hunt spear, but broader in
the blade, and with a stouter shaft. (Fig. F shows
the section.)

I need not add that all spears ought to be
made of the best tempered steel. With one

made by Thornhill, of Bond Street, I can drive
a hole through a dollar without turning the edge,
a sure proof that the best of " stuff" is used in
his factory.

A stout male bamboo, sufficiently tapering,
and with knots pretty close together, makes *the*
best spear-shaft ; but a close-grained, well-
seasoned ash-pole is not a bad substitute.

The spear ought to be well balanced, and it is
usual to have the butt weighted with lead for
that purpose. The spears of the Deccan and
Nugger Hunts were exactly 9 feet from the
extreme point to the butt, and this is, I consider,
the best length for general purposes.

In Bengal many sportsmen use a spear only 6
feet in length, heavily weighted at the butt.
They are accustomed to throw this like a javelin,
or to job down when the horse gets alongside of
the boar; whereas, in Madras and Bombay, hog-
hunters use the spear like a lance, but carried
loosely in the hand, so as to allow the free

play to the wrist in directing the point of the
spear.

Hunting
Cart.

In India, I had constructed, according to my own plan and fancy, what
I should advise every sportsman in that country
to possess—that is, a very comfortable teak-wood
bullock-cart, on springs, and fitted up for travelling or living in. Mine was 7 feet long by 4 feet
broad; and contained three large water-tight
boxes or compartments, to hold my kit and
comestibles *en route*, with a fourth, copper-lined
and fitted with a screw-top, which fastened with a
lock, for my ammunition, besides a rack for eight
guns. The wooden sides were about 2½ feet in
height, and from them sprang six bamboo hoops,
on which the white painted canvas top was extended; the whole of which gear was movable,
and could be cleared away at a moment's notice.
The bottom of the cart was slightly bevelled off
round, caulked and sheathed with copper; so
that, by taking out the linch-pins, and putting the
wheels into the cart, my trap served me as a boat

to transfer myself and goods across rivers otherwise impassable. When in cantonment I took
out the pole and bullock-yoke, and fitted in a
pair of shafts; and although it was not a very
light article, an Australian mare I had used
to trot along with it with great ease. The whole
length of the bottom of the cart was fitted with a
hair mattress, and the sides were well padded, so
that I managed, when travelling, to get along
pretty comfortably.

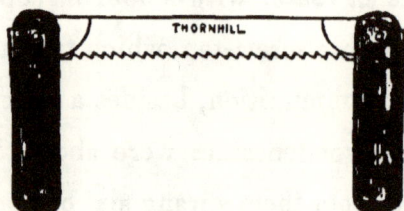

Thornhill's Saw.

Appurte-   A large Yankee backwoodsman's
nances.   axe, a couple of bill-hooks, an adze,
and other tools, were fitted against the side
of my cart, so as to be ready at hand in case
of a break-down, which is an event of frequent
occurrence in Indian travelling. An obstrepe-

rous bullock or a careless driver is very liable to
smash a pole or a yoke *en route;* and, in many
parts of the country where game abounds, village
smiths are difficult to be met with, and I have often
been saved hours and even days' delay, by having
the means of repairing them at hand.

Medicine
Chest.
A well-supplied medicine-chest, in
which the quinine-bottle loomed very
large, was carefully stowed away in one of the
compartments—a very necessary precaution in a
country where disease makes such rapid progress.
Besides having often found this chest extremely
useful, the mere fact of having it with me inspired
my people with confidence, and overcame their
fear of the malaria of the dense jungle.

Messrs. Savory and Moore, of 143, New Bond
Street, have always filled up my medicine-chest;
and their practical experience has been of the
greatest use to me in my travels, for, in case of
sickness, the proper remedy was ever at hand when
wanted. In order to meet different requirements,
large and small chests have been designed, from

the size of a pocket-book to the medical panniers
containing all appliances, both medical and surgical, that may be required by a regiment in the
field.

The following Plates illustrate those best
adapted for a traveller or sportsman:

The above Plate represents a strong leather case,
6 inches by 9 inches, and only 2½ inches in thickness (in fact, of the form and size of an ordinary
octavo volume, and opening in much the same
manner), contains a pair of scales, with the
necessary weights, a small glass measure, 8 small
bottles adapted to receive either powders or pills,
8 of larger size stoppered for liquids, and 2 still

larger for holding any medicines required in greater bulk. This little case, which would scarcely take up any appreciable room in the travelling bag, will contain all the medicines required in any case of emergency. Its value to a party of tourists, or to a single traveller, removed from medical aid, can hardly be over-rated. The " Special Correspondents" of our daily papers have used these cases in nearly every quarter of the globe, and have spoken most highly of their utility.

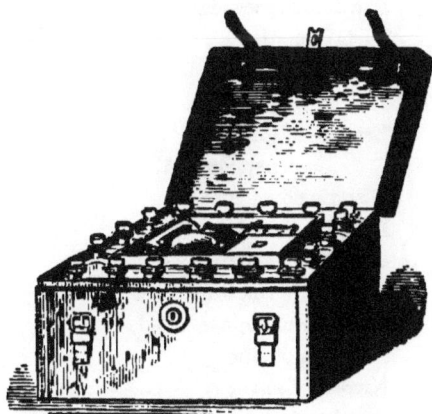

This Plate represents a larger case of the same character, containing a greater number of remedies, and, in addition, a few surgical appliances that may be required in an emergency.

List of Medicines suitable for a Medicine Chest for India or Abyssinia.

Quinine.
Calomel.
Jalap.
Rhubarb.
Magnesia.
Essence of camphor (rubini).
Tincture of iodine.
    „   arnica.
Mindererus spirit.
Sweet spirit of nitre.
Powdered ipecacuanha.
Tartar emetic.
James's powder.
Jeremie's opiate.
Essence of ginger.
    „   peppermint.
Dover's powder.
Friars' balsam.
Essence of senna.
Warburg's tincture.
Sulphate of copper.
Sulphate of zinc.
Nitrate of silver.
Opiate confection, tablets.
Aromatic confection,   „
Calomel and opium pills.
Etherodine (instead of chlorodyne).

Full information and directions respecting the administration of the various remedies will be found in the " Compendium of Domestic Medicine, and Companion to the Medicine Chest," by Savory and Moore, 143, New Bond Street.

The Filter. A filter is a most important requisite, which ought always to be found in a traveller's equipment, as good water is as essential to health as pure air.

The Danchell Pocket Filter.

.A very efficient portable filter is manufactured by the London and General Water Purifying

E

Company, at 157, Strand, being the invention of Mr. Danchell.

This filter, which is only 3 inches in diameter, is constructed upon the syphon principle, and by means of a system of ascending currents the suspended impurities are separately precipitated outside the filter, whilst those only which are held in solution actually pass into the filtering material, the water being purified from these in the act of ascension. A case of galvanised iron contains the filtering material—animal charcoal— which is the best medium for purifying, as it is incapable of communicating any taint to the water passing through it, retains its purifying properties for a long period, and is everywhere easily procurable.

The action of this system is so simple that no attention or trouble is required in its management; it never clogs up, and is so arranged that the animal charcoal is easily got at for cleansing or renewal.

Directions.

When the filter ceases to act satisfactorily, it may be detached from the pipe by unscrewing the union which is immediately above the cap of the filter, the filter taken out of the cistern, and the charcoal removed and cleansed, or replaced by new. To effect this the cap of the filter must be removed by knocking the claws of the iron holding the cap down, round on the graduated edge to the thinnest part of it, when the openings in the edge will allow the iron being taken off and the cap then removed from the filter. The strainer must then be removed, after which the charcoal must be shaken out.

To Cleanse the Charcoal. It should be left to soak in lukewarm water for a short time, which will free its surface of organic matter, and afterwards well washed in clean water. The water in which the charcoal is washed will always be black, and affords no guide to the charcoal being clean. After washing, the charcoal must be dried and sifted into two portions—No. 1, the very coarse; No. 2, the remainder.

To Refill the Filter. First put in No. 1 (the very coarse charcoal) to the depth of 1 or 1½ inches; then the body of the charcoal, No. 2, may be put in, the filter being kept in constant motion by raising it a little on one side, and allowing it to receive a slight downward jerk on whatever it may be standing, the filter being turned occasionally to ensure the motion being equally distributed. By this means a much larger body of charcoal may be got in, for after being apparently full many times it will be found still capable of holding more. The last 1 or 2 inches should be the remainder of No. 1 charcoal. The strainer must be then replaced by agitating the filter as before described, and pressing it upon the charcoal, which will cause the charcoal to gather well round the strainer. The cap and rubber-washer must be fixed as before, the iron claw knocked round carefully with a mallet to its original position, and it is ready for use.

A very excellent pocket syphon-filter weighing only 8 ounces, somewhat on the same principle, is also made by Messieurs Atkins and Sons, 62, Fleet Street, when the water is purified by passing through a block of moulded carbon, which is made perfectly porous but not hollow.

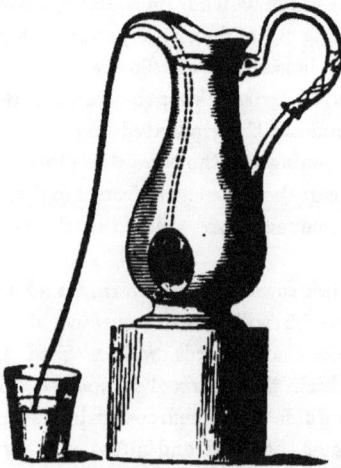

Syphon Filter.

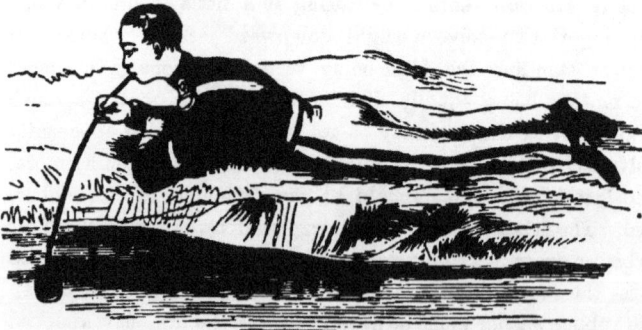

Atkins' Pocket Filter.

Directions. These blocks will get clogged sooner or later ;
and the frequency of cleaning them depends upon
the nature of the water filtered, some waters clogging the carbon
sooner than others. They are, however, easily cleaned by simply
washing them in hot water, brushing them with a soft brush,
and, finally, blowing through them two or three times, to open
the pores. When cleaned, they are equal to new, as only the
surface gets clogged. When the operation of filtering is over,
the ball should be blown through, to clear the pores from the
impurities, and put away in the case as dry as possible.

When cattle have to be watered from a well,
or from holes dug in the sandy bed of a river,
which is often the case in African travelling,
having to bale out the water is an intolerable
nuisance. I therefore devised the following
arrangement, which Mr. Atkins, of 62, Fleet
Street, has carried out most effectually.

Into the well or pool I drop a filter, which is
kept a foot or more below the surface by a float ;
to this is connected a tube or suction hose attached to a small portable force pump, by
which I draw the pure water from the well,
and force it into a trough from which the cattle
drink.

By this system the water in the pool remains

" The Old Shekarry's" Pump and Filter combined.

undisturbed and clear, whilst if cattle were allowed to rush into it to drink, the mud would be stirred up, and the water rendered unfit for drinking until after it had settled.

Were Government to adopt some such system in watering cavalry horses, etc., much trouble and inconvenience would be avoided, whilst the animals would thrive all the better for having filtered and pure water to drink.

Cording's Inflatable India-Rubber Boat.

Cording's India-Rubber Boat. This invention has proved invaluable to sportsmen and travellers, as a boat of this description is very portable,

and stands a great deal of wear and tear in any
climate.

For crossing or going down a river, they are
all that can be desired; but it is almost impossible to paddle them up stream or against a
head-wind, as they float so high out of the water.

CHAPTER III.

ARMAMENT.

PART I.—SPORTING ARMS.

A Sportsman's Battery—Westley Richards' Breech-Loading System, as applied to Sporting Arms—The Pin and Central-Fire Cartridges compared—The Introduction of the Breech-Loading System into England—Thirty Reasons for preferring Breech-Loading Guns and Rifles—The Disadvantages of the Muzzle-Loading System—The Gun Case and its Appurtenances—Machines for Loading Cartridges—Cartridge Belts—Cartridge Magazines—Cartridge Carriers—Game Carriers.

SUCCESS in "the field," whether in battle or at the covert side, in a great measure depends upon the armament.

A sportsman, explorer, or officer, proceeding on service to the Colonies, to be properly equipped, ought to have the following arms:

1. A Double-Barrel Breech-Loading Gun, 12 bore.
2. A Double-Barrel Breech-Loading Rifle, 12 bore,
3. A Double-Barrel Breech-Loading Holster Pistol.
4. A Revolver for his Belt.

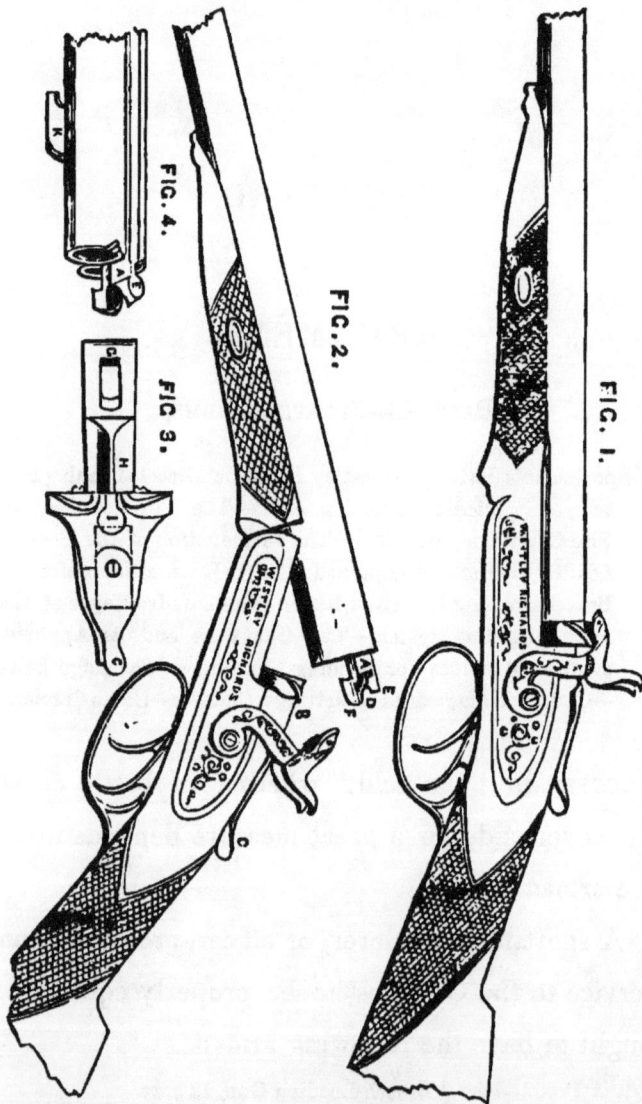

Breech-loading Double Gun, on Westley Richards' System.

For sporting purposes, I consider the best breech-loading system, both for guns and rifles, to be that of Mr. Westley Richards; as its construction is a wonderful combination of strength and simplicity, and it is in every way preferable to any other system I have yet seen, " and their name is legion."

A gun or rifle, on this system, is very similar in outward appearance, to an ordinary muzzle-loader, having bar or front-action locks, and the grip or fore-part being of wood. (*Vide* Plate, page 58, Figs. 1 and 2.)

The mechanical arrangement (*vide* Plate) is of a most safe and simple character. A self-acting spring latch (*b, c,* Fig. 2) secures the breech-end of the barrels, fitting into the solid iron after loading. The barrels are released by a simple action of the thumb, and the loading is effected with the greatest ease.

The barrels are secured to the body of the gun by fastenings, both at the top and bottom, thus disposing of the strength to the greatest possible advantage; whereas other systems of breech-loaders have only one fastening, and that considerably below the centre or point of resistance.

The connecting-piece between the barrels is a solid lump of steel (*a*), which, when the barrels are closed, dovetails on to the break-cff (*i*, Fig. 3), and holds the two firmly together like a solid piece. Besides this improvement, that arm has a *solid joint* (as shown at *g*, Fig. 3, and *k*, Fig. 4), which is infinitely stronger than the ordinary fastening, made with a loose pin screwed through the ends of the body; and it has also a keel, or wedge (*h*, in Fig. 3), fitting between the under part of the action, which adds strength to the stock.

The shooting of Mr. Westley Richards' guns and rifles *is all that can be desired*, as the invariable success he has met with at Wimbledon and in the Gun Club contests proves. In finish and durability they are not to be surpassed.

For sporting purposes I much prefer the pin cartridge system (*vide* Plate, page 61, Fig. *a*,) to what is called the central fire* (*vide* Plate below, Fig. *b*), for the following reasons:

First.—Without an indicator, which is constantly getting out of order, it is impossible to

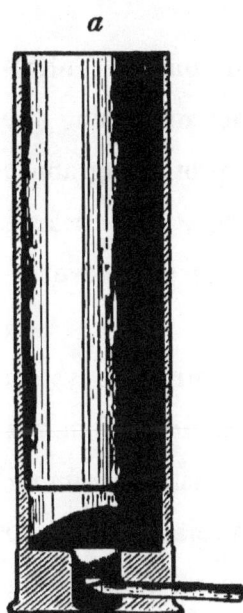

SECTION OF PIN CARTRIDGE CASE.

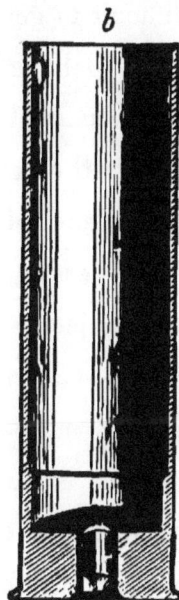

SECTION OF CENTRAL-FIRE CASE.

know whether a gun is loaded or not, and accidents might happen from this cause.

---

* The ignition in the so-called central-fire cartridges is not more central or instantaneous than in the pin cartridge.

Secondly.—A cartridge extractor, which weakens the breech, and is a complication liable to get out of order, is absolutely required in this system, and even then the exploded cartridges are sometimes difficult to get out.

Thirdly.—I have known a gun on the central-fire system to explode in the act of closing the breech, from the percussion cap protruding above the brass plane of the cartridge, and striking against the needle, which in some guns, even at half-cock, projects slightly.

Fourthly.—Cartridges on the central-fire system are certainly more dangerous to load than pin cartridges, for should a grain of sand get under the cap, or if the cap should project above the brass plane of the cartridge, the act of ramming down the wads smartly might cause the percussion-powder to ignite and the cartridge to explode.

Fifthly.—Pin cartridges are in more general use, and can be bought all over the Continent, whilst those on the central-fire system are difficult to be got except in London.

The Introduction of the Breech-loading System.

My experience in breech-loading arms for sporting purposes dates back since the year 1855, when my attention was attracted to the La Faucheux system,* which is almost as great an era in gun-making as the invention of the copper cap. After two years' experience and repeated trials, in which, to my disgust, I found my favourite Manton, and others of my hardest-hitting muzzle-loading guns, equalled or beaten by breech-loaders, my scepticism vanished; I felt convinced the system was sound, and that sooner or later a complete revolution must take place in the manufacture of fire-arms.

Under these impressions I endeavoured to concentrate my ideas on paper, for the benefit of my brother sportsmen, and my letter appeared

---

* Although this system was invented and extensively adopted in France several years previous to its introduction in this country, the French workmanship of that day was, generally speaking, so inferior, that no sportsman liked to shoot with a French gun. Even French sportsmen preferred English fire-arms.

in *The Field, the Country Gentleman's News-paper*, of the 31st October, 1857, in which I enumerated thirty advantages that breech-loaders possess over ordinary muzzle-loading guns. Little did I dream of "the hornets' nest" in which this innovation placed me. I was attacked on all sides, by gun-makers, book-makers, and contumacious, pedantic old sportsmen, who all declared forsooth, "that the Old Shekarry must be demented to think of adopting French fads and foreign gimcracks." However, that party (whose motto is *Frangas non flectes*) being some-what remarkable for pertinacity in his opinions, and inflexibility of purpose,* continued to dis-seminate his doctrine in spite of the sarcastic

---

* The Old Shekarry, when a very small boy, went with his Maternal to have his bumps felt. The phrenologist, a quaint old card, went on with his work in a very matter-of-fact style until he came to a protuberance which seemed to puzzle him; he grunted, felt again, and then speaking to the boy who wrote to his dictation, said : "No. 16. Firmness—immoderately large," (*sotto voce* to the Maternal), "amounting, I am afraid, madam, to obstinacy." The old lady, who, up to that time, had enter-tained doubts as to the truthfulness of phrenology, went home quite a convert.

insinuations of tribes of gun-sellers, who, doubt-
less, had large stocks of muzzle-loaders on hand,
and did not like to see the value of their stock
go down in the market. " The system is not
safe; the breech is not sound; the guns will not
shoot; " was the cry, and at times the controversy
became so warm, that the " interested oppo-
nents " became even unparliamentary in their
language.

Bets of all descriptions, to any amount, were
offered, which, had the Old Shekarry been " an
army contractor" instead of a soldier, he would
have had to borrow capital to cover. At this
crisis, General Charitée, a celebrated old sportsman and a crack shot, came to the rescue, chal-
lenged all comers in *The Field*, and offered to
back his breech-loader, made by Lang, for a
thousand pounds, against any muzzle-loader be-
longing to the boisterous crew. This plucky
offer, although never taken up, hushed the storm,
the agitation was calmed, temperate discussion
followed, trials were organised, the subject was

F

ventilated, and, as a matter of course, the breech-loading system became a recognised institution in the sporting world.

I have now used the breech-loader for twelve years, during which time I have shot a great deal in the worst climate for arms of any description (the West Coast of Equatorial Africa), and, after giving the system every trial that experience can devise, I have found no reason to alter my opinion as to its excellence and efficiency.

Thirty Reasons for preferring the Breech-loading System.

The thirty reasons why I prefer the breech-loader to the ordinary muzzle-loader, which I gave in *The Field* newspaper in 1857, are—

Quickness of Loading.

1. The extreme facility and quickness in the loading, whereby any person with a breech-loader may load and fire at least six shots in the same time that another with a common gun takes to load and fire two.

2. Whilst shooting with a party in line, what a decided advantage the breech-loader has over

the common gun! No halting the line to reload; you fire, and continue moving on, loading with the greatest ease and celerity as you go. By this means the line is kept unbroken, and in cover the sportsmen are not exposed to the danger of a stray shot from any one lagging behind. What is more calculated to try the patience of a man than this continual stopping? No one likes to keep his friends waiting, and consequently reloads with the greatest expedition. In the hurry of the moment how often does a shot drop in the nipple, or some mistake take place in the loading? to rectify which the line is delayed, and the game, perhaps already afoot, makes off. All this is avoided by the breech-loader.

Safety in Loading.
3. The great comparative safety in using a breech-loader is undeniable. Never by any chance need you have the direction of your gun's muzzle pointed either towards yourself or your friends in loading. It should be kept in the direction you are going.

4. You cannot make any mistake in the loading,

such as leaving out or putting in two charges of powder or shot into one barrel.

5. How many accidents have taken place from a sportsman, in the haste or excitement of the moment, loading one barrel with the other on full cock, which the shock of ramming tight wads, or catching in the trousers or a twig, has caused to go off! There is no chance of this with a breech-loader.

6. How many accidents does one hear of taking place with the common gun, from the pouring powder from a full flask down to the muzzle of a gun recently discharged, in which perhaps a bit of lighted tow, or, what is oftener the case, a bit of cork (got in the powder in taking the cork out of the canister) may remain. There is no chance of losing a hand in this manner with a breech-loader.

Accidents Impossible. 7. You are always enabled whilst loading to see clearly through your barrels, and are certain, each shot, that there is no obstruction or dirt got in, which is a great advantage, as many people have been injured by guns bursting from the muzzle being accidentally plugged up with clay, which may have got in whilst jumping a ditch, climbing over a fence, or stumbling on an uneven turnip-field.

8. From the formation of the cartridge, your shot cannot loosen or fall out whilst walking with the muzzle downwards.

9. You have no chance of the nipple breaking, or being bothered with its stopping up.

Advantages whilst Shooting. 10. How often in a day's shooting, when both barrels are discharged, do you mark a bird down: what an advantage the sportsman armed with a breech-loader has, in being enabled to walk up at once, loading as he goes, without ever taking his eyes from off the spot where the game settled!

Absence of Flash. 11. Among other advantages is the total absence of any flash or escape from the breech. Thus, in firing the second barrel on a damp day, the sight is not obstructed, from smoke hanging before the eyes.

12. There is much less report from a breech-

loader than from an ordinary gun, from the whole
discharge taking place internally.

13. There is no chance of some unlucky cap
flying, and endangering your eyesight.

Less Recoil.

14. There is very much less recoil
than from an ordinary gun—a great
advantage in a long day's shooting; no blackened
shoulders, no stiffness the day after. The reason
of there being less recoil in a breech-loader than
in a muzzle-loader of the same size and weight, is
that its construction renders it necessary to have
more weight of metal at the breech; and also
because at the hollow of the cartridge of the
breech-loader there is a light roll of paper,
about one-eighth of an inch in thickness, which
(like the buffer of a railway carriage) gives
with the action of the powder, and lessens the
recoil.

Not affected
by Weather.

15. Rain or damp, whilst out shooting, cannot affect or injure the charge
or caps; neither being exposed to the weather, in
the same way the nipple of the ordinary gun is.

No chance of miss-fires on that account with a breech-loader.

Cleaning. 16. The breech-loader takes very little time to clean; a piece of tow and an oiled rag run through the barrel is sufficient; and by looking through them, it is very easy to be seen whether they are clean—a great advantage. Whereas, with an ordinary gun, by the act of reloading, the dirt and *débris* of the last discharge is forced into the breech or the nipple, and frequent washing out of the barrels is required.

No Second Gun required. 17. The carrying out of a second gun is obviated; for a sportsman can reload his gun in most cases more quickly than his keeper can hand him another. I have always had an objection to having a keeper walking behind me with a loaded gun. Perhaps it may be a weakness I have; but I always feel afraid of his stumbling, and " making game " of me.

Less to Carry. 18. The bother of carrying powder-flask, shot-bag, caps, wads, loading-rod, and nipple-

screw is avoided; none being required with a
breech-loader, the cartridges being carried either
in the pocket or in a waist-belt.

Quickness in   19. Breech-loaders shoot *quicker*
Shooting.   than muzzle-loaders, because there is
no long communication (the nipple) between the
point of ignition and the charge, the explosion of
the cap taking place in the centre of the powder,
which is inflamed *almost* simultaneously; for it
is an error to suppose even that gunpowder explodes instantaneously, as, however rapid its progress, it takes a certain time in travelling from
the first grain to the last.

Foul very   20. Breech-loaders *foul very little*,
Little.   as the thick elastic mercurial waddings
which enter the breech are fully a size larger
than the bore of the muzzle; consequently, being
driven through the barrel by the action of the
powder, each discharge carries away any refuse
or accumulation that may have been left by the
previous one, and at the end of a long day's
shooting the barrel is almost as free from foul-

ness as at the beginning; also, the explosion
of the charge does not take place in the breech,
but in the paper cartridge, which comes out
uninjured, containing the *débris* of the burnt
powder, which in the ordinary gun is drawn into
the chamber and nipple every time it is reloaded,
until the latter becomes clogged up, and miss-
fires are the consequence.

Advantages
whenLoad-
ing.
21. What an advantage it is, when
shooting in fens, swamps, or rice fields,
to be able to load without being obliged to put
the butt of your gun in the mud or water,
whereby you wet and soil your clothes when
you put it up to the shoulder, making yourself
uncomfortable for the day.

22. When shooting in dense covers, or perhaps
when perched in the fork of a tree, or in a pit
waiting by water, or a salt-lick for deer, bison, or
other large game, what an advantage it is being
able to reload with so very little change of
position in a small space !

23. What an advantage to the Indian sports-

man who fires and reloads in a howdah, moving and shaking from the motion of the elephant!

24. What an advantage to the elephant-hunter in South Africa, who is obliged to load and fire from his horse's back; having to keep his eye perhaps on an infuriated wounded animal, to look out for obstructions in his path, and to reload his discharged piece.

25. How often in the field does the noise of ramming down a tight wad, whilst reloading the ordinary gun, put up birds on all sides, who thus get away, to the sportsman's disgust! Not so with the breech-loader. What an advantage being able to load without noise is to the snipe-shooter, who often, after a hard day's blank fag, arrives on small insulated patches of grass alive with snipe, where he may perhaps fire a dozen shots without moving a single pace, and when every slightest movement and noise, caused by reloading, puts up dozens of birds all round, whom he has the mortification of hearing call "Scape, scape!" as they collect in clouds and soar away. When

birds are thick, I fairly believe, all things considered, that a sportsman armed with a breech-
loader may easily kill twice as many birds as an
equal shot with a common gun.

26. What sportsman, after a heavy day's
snipe-shooting under a hot sun, has not found
his hands all sore and blistered, from constantly
ramming down the charge? Never this with
a breech-loader. What an advantage this is
to the engineer officer, who has often in India
to give up the amusement of snipe-shooting,
because it makes his hands unfit to use the
pen.

27. Who does not feel that he can shoot better
and with greater satisfaction, having his hands
clean? whereas with a common gun they will in
a few times loading get blackened with exploded
powder, and sticky. Now, with a breech-loader,
a man may put on a pair of white kid gloves,
kill a good bag of game, and return with them
scarcely soiled.

28. In cold weather, who has not found the

loading of a common gun and putting on caps
distress him beyond measure, especially if he has
been obliged to pull off his warm gloves before
he is able to effect it at last? No such bother
with a breech-loader.

Ease in chang-
ing Charge.
29. What an advantage it is being
able to draw your charge in a moment,
and change the number of your shot. How
often whilst after snipe do you come across duck;
or, whilst after hares and partridges, do you start
a herd of deer, a sounder of pig, or perhaps a
royal tiger?

30. How pleasant it is being able to substitute
ball for shot in a few seconds, instead of the old
tedious manner of drawing your charge with
the screw of your ramrod, which takes ten times
as long, and makes noise enough to scare away
the game.

The sportsman can easily make up his own
cartridges at the rate of about half-a-gross in an
hour; or, if he prefers it, he can purchase them
all ready from any gunmaker.

Old Preju-
dices. When all the advantages of the breech-loader are contrasted with the known disadvantages of the muzzle-loader, it is difficult to account for the prejudice that has existed against them for so many years; for, notwithstanding that the present system was introduced by La Faucheux a quarter of a century ago, it is only lately that it has come into general use amongst sportsmen. Numerous objections have been urged against the system, but none appear to have had any substantial foundation; and I shall not enter into them, although I am aware that there are many sportsmen of the old school who, from prejudice, will not even deign to give it a trial: with them, arguments and facts are both equally lost.

The Disadvan-
tages of the
Muzzle-load-
ing System. In the pursuit of large game, breech-loading arms are infinitely preferable; for until the last few years the hunter was always obliged, when waging war with the denizens of the forest, to keep up a battery of several guns and rifles, which, to say nothing of

the expense of the first outlay and the continual
wear and tear, etc., was attended by several serious
disadvantages, some half-dozen of which I shall
enumerate.

In the first place, two or three gun-bearers
are required to each sportsman, whose duty it is
to pass up the spare guns as fast as those in hand
are discharged; now, it is a great disadvantage
for a hunter, when on trail or stalking, to have
a number of persons at his heels, on account of
the extra noise they must necessarily make in
forcing their way through cover, which often
gives alarm to the game, and prevents him from
getting a shot.

Secondly, it is a great drawback, whilst in the
pursuit of some dangerous animal, when a *faux
pas* might be attended with fatal consequences, to
have any other than yourself to look after.

Thirdly, it is not pleasant to have loaded fire-
arms carried in the rear by inexperienced hands,
with whom an accident from carelessness is as
likely to occur as not.

Fourthly, it is not a comfortable feeling to have to depend upon the coolness and courage of your followers; and many a sportsman has found himself in an awkward position by his gun-bearers having been seized with a panic, and bolting, leaving him, with both barrels discharged, in the presence of a wounded and infuriated animal, when nothing but some lucky chance can prevent a catastrophe.

Fifthly, it frequently happens, in hunting in different countries, that the sportsman (if he does not keep in his pay a shekar-gang of his own, which is expensive work) has to entrust his spare guns to men of whom he knows nothing, who may be tempted to decamp with them—not a very unfrequent occurrence.*

Sixthly, it is a great annoyance to a tired sportsman, after a hard day's fag, to have to clean four or five double guns and rifles, which task he

---

* Lieut. Rice, of the Bombay Army, lost all his guns in this manner.

dare not entrust his followers to perform, as there are times when a miss-fire might be attended with the most serious consequences.

Happily for the sportsmen of the present day, all these disagreeable contingencies may now be avoided by making use of rifles on the breech-loading system. Now, independent of gun-bearers, he can roam through the forest alone, careless as to what animal he may meet, for he knows that, should his first shots not take deadly effect, he can reload in the twinkling of an eye, and keep up a running fire, against which no-thing can stand, instead of having to bolt under cover to reload (in case a spare gun is not at hand), returning breathless, and often with un-steady hand, from having to use sheer force in jamming an obstinate ball down a foul barrel. When mounted, a rifle on the breech-loading system has immense advantages, as it can be easily reloaded, without in any way interfering with the management of the horse; whereas with the old muzzle-loader the sportsman was

entirely powerless whilst drawing his ramrod
and ramming home the bullet. He who has
once used a breech-loading gun or rifle will no
more think of going back to a muzzle-loader
than the crack marksman at Hythe would return
to old " Brown Bess."

Jacobs' Shells. Percussion shells invented by Captain
Norton and improved by General
Jacobs, are often used by sportsmen when shooting
large game. They consist of copper cases, full
of gunpowder, encased in a leaden cylindro-conical projectile, at the apex of which is the point
of the shell containing percussion powder, that
explodes on striking any object. (*Vide* Plate.)

Section of Jacobs' Shell.   Jacobs' Shell.

These shells are very useful for riflemen when engaged with field artillery, as ammunition caissons may be blown up by them.

Case and Appurtenances. The best cases for guns or rifles are of solid leather, and they ought to be made as compact as possible. Messrs. Bussey and Co., of New Oxford Street, make most excellent cases, as well as all necessary accessories.

The Gun-Case (Plate, page 83, Fig. 1) usually contains :

The Barrel Cleaner, Fig. 2.
The Cartridge Loading Machine, Fig. 3.
Measures for Powder and Shot, Fig. 2, page 82; Fig 4, page 83.
A Cartridge Extractor, Fig. 1, page 82.
A Felt Breech-Cleaner.
A Cartridge-Carrier, Plate, page 86.
An Oil-Bottle, Lock-Brush, Scratch-Brush, and Turnscrew. .

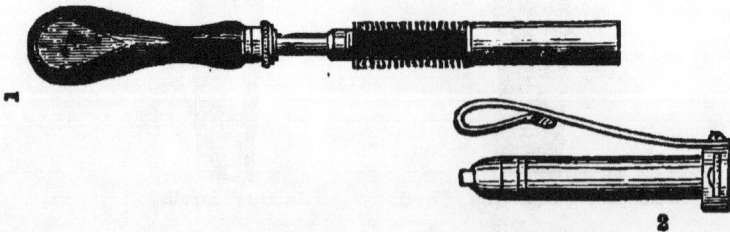

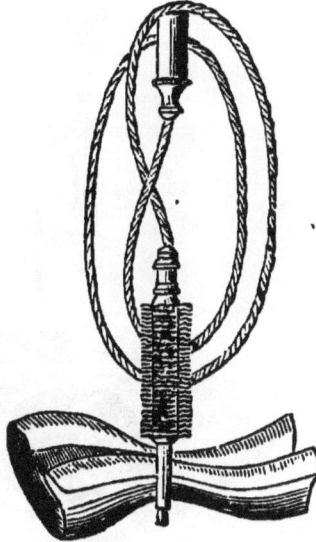

1   4   3

Gun-Case and Appurtenances.

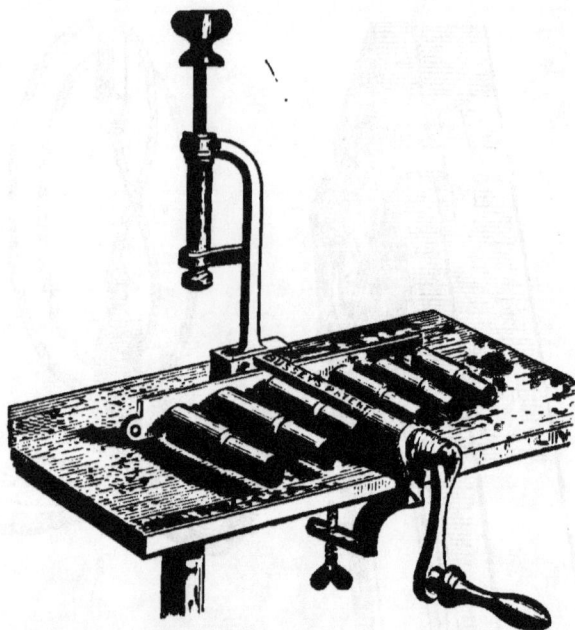

Machine for Loading Cartridges. "Bussey's Patent."

Sportsmen who load their own cartridges require a machine for the purpose. That invented by Mr. George Bussey is one of the best, as its construction is so simple that it can scarcely get out of order; the cartridges can be rapidly leaded, and it is so compact that it will fit into any ordinary gun-case.

Directions for Loading Cartridges.

1st. Screw the frame of the machine to a table very firmly.

2nd. Insert a case in each chamber of the holder, and close the lid.

3rd. Charge each case successively with powder, and then insert the six wads.

4th. Bring the holder parallel with the frame, taking care that the first cartridge is exactly under the plunger, drive down the wad by a blow on the plunger with the palm of the right hand, using the left to slide the holder along, and so bring each cartridge exactly under the plunger, till the six have been rammed home.

5th. Repeat the processes Nos. 3 and 4 for the shot.

6th. Now take the holder horizontally in the left hand, and submit each cartridge to the screw successively, after which they drop out of the chambers by turning the hinged lid of the holder.

To load quickly without spilling, the vessels containing the powder and shot should be just the height of the cartridge case (*i. e.*, about $2\frac{3}{4}$ inches.)

Any sportsman, with a little practice, may load 150 cartridges within the hour.

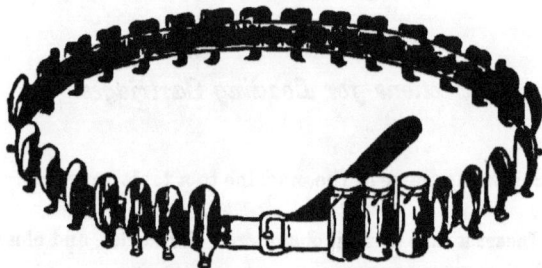

Spring Cartridge Belt. "Bussey's Patent."

The spring cartridge-belt, invented by Mr. George Bussey, is one of the best and most convenient yet introduced. It is worn under the coat and carries from 30 to 36 cartridges.

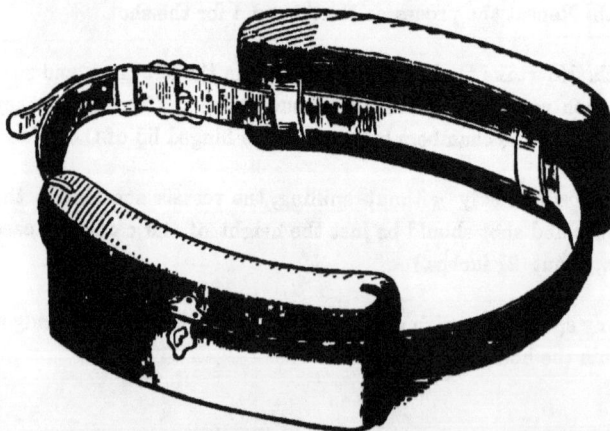

Cartridge Carrier.

Keeper's Cartridge Case. The foregoing shows the best kind of cartridge case for a keeper to carry reserve ammunition.

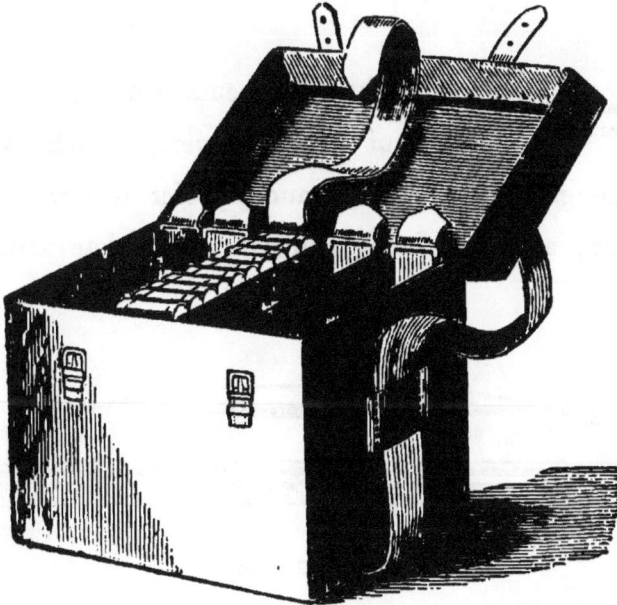

Magazine.

Cartridge Magazine. Loaded cartridges are best carried in a compact magazine, holding from 200 to 500, similar to the foregoing Plate, as it is fitted with regulating straps, which prevent the cartridges from being damaged by shaking about, as is too often the case with other methods of stowage.

Game Carriers.　The following cuts show the best kinds of game carriers, which, although very simple, I much prefer to nets and bags, as the air being allowed to circulate about

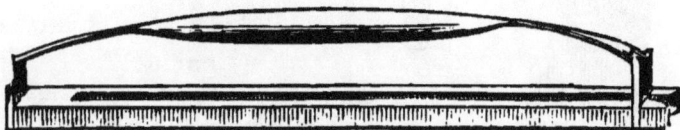

Game Carrier.

the game, it is kept cooler, and does not turn putrid so soon as it would do, if all huddled together in a bag. I like to have my game kept long enough to become tender, but, not.

being of the vulture tribe, do not fancy decomposed meat.

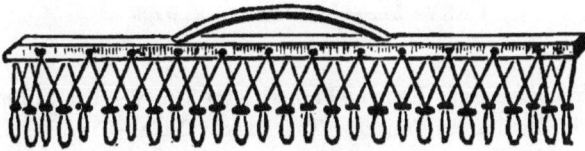

CHAPTER IV.

ARMAMENT.

PART II.—MILITARY ARMS.

The Importance of " Keeping Pace with the Times"—Brown Bess
—The Percussion Musket—The Enfield Rifle—The Westley
Richards' Breech-loading Rifle and Cartridge—The Westley
Richards' Central Fire Military Rifle and Cartridge—The Snider
Rifle and the Boxer Cartridge—Different Systems of Rifling
compared—Holster Pistols—Colt's Repeating Arms—Dean's
Revolver—Tranter's Breech-loading Revolver—"The Whis-
perer"—Breech-loading Mountain Guns—Jacobs' Shells.

AT last, in spite of the trammels of red tape
and old-fashioned official routine, " the powers
that be" have become aware of the fact, that in
order to maintain our national prestige they must
keep pace with the times; and although Government are still very slow in recognising real merit
in new inventions, and look upon every contem-

plated change as an officious innovation, still much has been done to benefit the service, more especially as regards the armament of our land and sea forces, and one of the most efficient reforms has been the adoption of the Snider breech-loader.

Brown Bess. One of the greatest generals of the past, Sir Charles J. Napier, the conqueror of Scinde, believed in the efficiency of the old Brown Bess of his day with its flint-lock and bright barrel; for he had seen many a glorious field won by men armed only with that weapon, and knew no other.

The Percussion Musket. The first great change for the better was the introduction of the percussion musket, which was regarded with such suspicion by the authorities, that, in the first instance, I remember only one company per regiment was entrusted with it. Time passed, and the new arms did good execution in their day, for with them the decisive battles of the Sutlej and the Punjab were won.

The Enfield Rifle.

Thanks, however, to the late Duke of Newcastle, then Secretary of State for War, and the right man in the right place, in spite of the tenaciousness of ancient prejudices, the *grooved bore* was issued to the line, first the Minié, and subsequently the Enfield; and this country is indebted to that wise minister for the most brilliant victory of modern times, as it was solely by the deadly efficiency of their volleys that a handful of British troops were enabled to hold their own, and repulse overpowering numbers of a brave and determined enemy on the heights of Inkerman.

Breech-loading Rifles adopted.

Ten years have rolled on since that murky morning when the soldiers' battle was won, and another era in our national armament is at hand, for the weapon that did us such good service at Inkerman has been discarded, and Government are arming the whole of our army and navy with breech-loaders.

The repeated warnings of the press, to whom be all honour for its wise foresight and unceasing watchfulness over the safety and honour of the country, together with the sad results of the late Danish and Austrian campaigns, have done much to open the eyes of the authorities, and make them aware, that even the bravest of troops, equipped with antiquated weapons, cannot hold the most defensible positions against the attack of an enemy whose arms combine every improvement of the age.

It is to be hoped that these unfortunate campaigns will serve as a warning to future ministers, and prevent any false economy, old prejudices, red-tape, or procrastinating official routine interfering with the effective maintenance of our national defences, and the efficient equipment of our land and sea forces, according to the march of the age, and the improvements that science is continually making. If Great Britain is to be maintained as a first-class power, she must, as in days of yore, ever be prepared against an emergency. Her supremacy was won by force of arms, and by force of arms it must be kept. The time has not come for the sword to be turned into a ploughshare; and as we wish for peace, we should be prepared for war.

Diplomacy, although useful in its way, should not be our sole dependence when the honour, safety, and liberty of action of the country are concerned. As a nation, we are not famous in that line—it never was our *forte*. We have often lost by treaties the advantages gained by the sacrifice of our best blood; for, whenever a question has arisen, our diplomatists have found their match; and the nation has had to fall back upon that which has never failed her—the staunch hearts and bull-dog courage of her stalwart sons.

Westley Richards' Breech-loading Cavalry Carbine.

This excellent arm [which has been adopted for some years in the cavalry, and of which Government have over 20,000 in store] is extremely simple and uncomplicated in construction, does not easily get out of order, and, in case of accident, can easily be repaired by a regimental armourer.

It can be loaded with great rapidity with the impossibility of any accident occurring, does not foul after heavy firing, is of great penetration, and, at long ranges, great accuracy of shooting can be obtained.

The total absence of foulness was satisfactorily proved by the experiments made by Government, when several hundred rounds were fired from this system without cleaning, and there was no more foulness in the barrel or greater recoil experienced in the last shot than the second.

This is easily accounted for, as the greased wad that lubricates the barrel at every discharge is of two sizes larger than the diameter of the barrel at the muzzle; consequently, whatever remains of the exploded powder or paper from the cartridge of the last shot is driven out of the barrel by the succeeding one.

For seven years in succession the chief prizes for breech-loading arms have been carried off by Mr. Westley Richards' rifles, which proves their extreme accuracy of shooting.

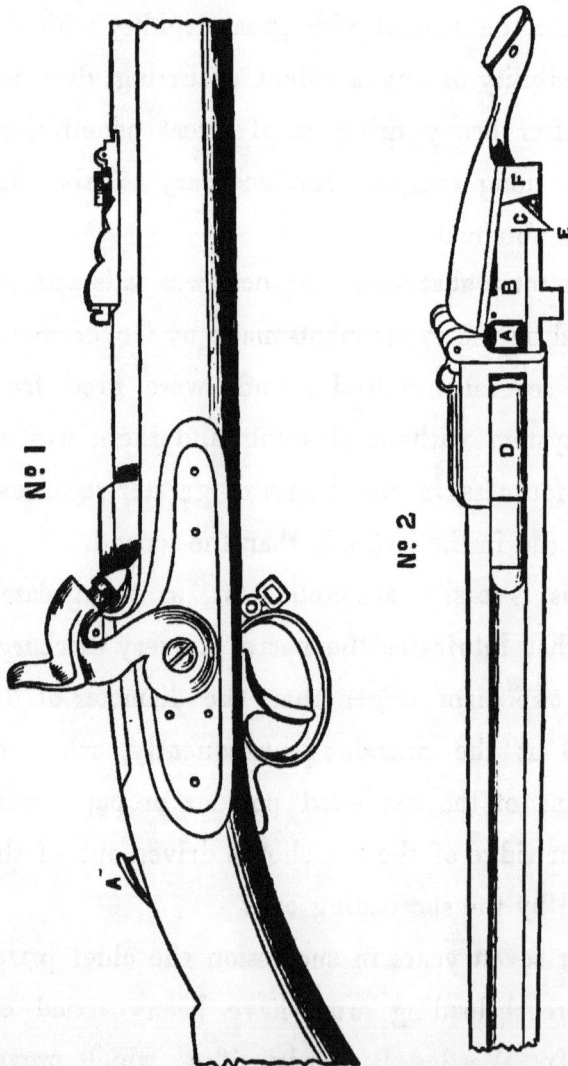

The Regulation Breech-loading Cavalry Carbine, on
Westley Richards' System.

The Plate on page 96, Fig. 1, represents the rifle closed. The small lump marked *a* is the only projecting part; in all other respects, the arm has the appearance of an ordinary rifle.

Fig. 2 represents a section of the breech-loading parts.

A is a gun-metal plunger which enters the breech-end of the gun.

B is a solid iron block, with an inclined plane at the back c.

There is a second inclined plane at the point E; this throws the block B back into its place, and makes it fit close against the end of the box F, which is also undercut, to fit the inclined part of the block B, at the point c. The block has a sliding motion to allow this action to take place.

By this it will be seen that the greater the pressure on the block and plunger, the safer the part becomes; the inclined plane holding the lever firmly down in its place.

D represents the cartridge.

H

Westley
Richards'
Central Fire
Military
Rifle.
Mr. Westley Richards has also invented a most excellent central-fire military breech-loading rifle, containing the ignition in the cartridge, which promises to supersede all other systems. But notwithstanding that the Duke of Cambridge's prize for breech-loading arms had been won for seven years in succession with rifles of his manufacture, he withdrew it from competition at the late Wimbledon meeting this year, because Mr. Henry's rifle, which is not a military arm, was put in competition with it.

Compared with the Snider Enfield, it has the advantage of being considerably lighter. The Snider Enfield and sixty rounds of ammunition weighing 2¼ lbs. heavier than Westley Richards' rifle and its sixty rounds.

For rapidity of fire it cannot be surpassed, as twenty shots per minute can easily be fired with it; and its accuracy of shooting is the same as that of his well-known breech-loader, which superseded the Terry rifle in the Services, and has

Westley Richards' Central Fire Military Rifle.

carried off the first breech-loading prize every
year in succession since the Wimbledon meeting

H 2

was established in 1860, and which up to this time has never been beaten.

The Plate on page 99 illustrates the system; and by comparing it with the Plate on page 96, it will be seen that the action is in many respects similar to Mr. Westley Richards' former rifle, the chief difference being that the sliding plunger (Plate, *aa*) is perforated, and contains a needle, or rather striker, *bb*, that receives the blow of the hammer, *d*, upon a projecting head, *c*, and which, sliding forward, explodes the cap contained in the felt wad (*vide* Plate, page 102), attached to the cartridge.

These felt wads are, after the insertion of the caps, dipped in tallow, and, by a very simple arrangement, a portion of this valuable lubricating agent is driven back by the side of the striker after each discharge, coming out through a hole in the side of the plunger, in regular rotation, and keeping every part in good working order.

A very ingenious lever, *e*, drives back the striker when the action is opened, by lifting up the arm, *f*, and thus all danger of an explosion is removed when the plunger is depressed.

There is no spring in the whole action, which is simple, uncomplicated, and in no way liable to get out of order.

Upwards of 10,000 rounds have been fired out of one of these rifles without cleaning, scarcely ever missing fire, and the arm is still serviceable and fit for work.

Its accuracy of shooting is 7·10 inches at 600 yards, which is all that can be desired.

These cartridges are so simple in their construction that, in case of need, soldiers can easily make them.

The Plate on page 102, Fig. 1, shows the cartridge as ready for insertion into the rifle, whilst Fig. 2 is a section of the same.

Fig. 3, showing the action of the ignition, is twice the size of the Government bore.

G, the striker or needle, strikes the head of an

Westley Richards' Cartridge.

ordinary percussion cap, *b*, against the point of an iron anvil, *a*, which is confined in its position by a copper broad-flanged cap, *c c c c*, at the extremity of which there is an aperture, *h h*, through which the flame is driven which ignites the charge, *f f.*

D d is a soft thick wad, *e e* a thin hard one, which are sown together, and keep the flanged cap, *c c*, and its contents in position.

The whole arrangement is very simple, and there is scarcely any possibility of a miss-fire.

The " Boxer" Cartridge. Eley Brothers are now manufacturing these cartridges under the Patent of Colonel Boxer, R.A., of Woolwich Arsenal, for Snider and other systems of breech-loading rifles taking central fire cartridges of ·577 and ·451 bore, they having been adopted by Government for use with the converted Snider Breech-loading Rifle.

The inventor states that they possess the following advantages :

"BOXER"
CARTRIDGE,
·577 BORE.

SECTION OF
"BOXER"
CARTRIDGE,
·577 BORE.

1. The principle of construction admits of such a difference between the size of the chamber and that of the cartridge, that no rough usage, to which the ammunition is liable, can interfere with facility of loading.

2. The withdrawal of the empty case is effected with perfect ease, even under adverse circumstances.

3. It cannot possibly swell by damp.

4. It may be crushed or disfigured to almost any extent, without danger of breakage or escape of gas.

5. It is practically waterproof, that is to say, it will withstand exposure to damp for almost any period, and it may be completely immersed in water for some time without injury.

6. It is not liable to deterioration from the effects of climate in any part of the world.

7. It is sure of ignition.

8. It is not liable to explosion in bulk; that is to say, the ignition of one or more cartridges will not extend to the remainder, indeed, a quantity of loose powder may be exploded in the centre of a barrel of ammunition without igniting any of the cartridges.

9. It excels in accuracy of shooting.

10. It is not liable to foul the rifle even under the most adverse circumstances.

The superior qualities of the Boxer cartridge have been fully established by the results of a series of experiments made by the Government. In these trials, the accuracy of shooting was better than that with the muzzle-loading ammunition, and only three miss-fires occurred out of the 10,000 rounds fired.

The fouling from 1000 consecutive rounds did not appreciably affect the accuracy of shooting or facility of loading.

After the cartridges had been immersed for six days in very wet sawdust no miss-fires occurred, and the loading was performed with the greatest ease in every case. The cartridges were bent, indented, and injured in various ways, without affecting the ease of loading or accuracy of shooting; they were shaken loose in a soldier's pouch for a month, and came out perfectly serviceable, and they were subjected to different atmospheric conditions artificially created without sustaining any injury.

As regards the safety of the Boxer cartridge, Captain Majendie, in his lecture at the R. U. S. Institution, stated as follows:

" I have several times exploded one cartridge in a barrel without igniting the remainder. I have fired ten at once, and no more exploded. I have gone further, and placed a barrel of 700 cartridges inside an iron cylinder tightly screwed down, and have exploded a quarter of a pound of powder in the midst, and although the screws were broken and the lid blown off with violence, and some of the cartridges strangely distorted, not a single cartridge was ignited."

To obviate any danger of these cartridges exploding accidentally by rough usage in transit, the anvil and chamber are purposely arranged so that they can scarcely be ignited except by a properly constructed rifle. Cartridges made to ignite very easily are extremely dangerous, being liable to explode when closing the rifle, in addition to the chance of ignition in transit.

Rifling.

Arms are still in a transition state, and it is yet a matter of doubt as to which system of rifling is the best.

From the numerous experiments I
have made and witnessed, I consider
that, for *accuracy of fire*, nothing equals that
of Mr Joseph Whitworth, of Manchester;
his rifle with the *hexagonal bore* and elongated projectile having "distanced" every
other at long ranges in the course of expe-
rimental trials lately made at the School of
Musketry at Hythe; besides which *the trajectory
is lower than any other system.* He uses a short
barrel, having an hexagonal bore and a very
quick turn; for whereas the Enfield rifle has
only one turn in 6 ft. 6in., and therefore only half
a turn in the barrel of the Enfield, which is 3 ft.
3 in., he has a 45-inch bore, with one turn in
20 inches, which rotation is sufficient with a
bullet of the requisite specific gravity. Mr.
Whitworth has reached such a pitch of accuracy,
that in a shed excluded from the influence of
wind, and firing from a beautifully-contrived
rest, at 500 yards he can put any number of con-

secutive balls within a space less than that occupied by a five-shilling piece; and it is said that he will not be contented until he can throw a bullet from the barrel of one rifle into the barrel of another placed at 500 yards' distance. His ordinary rifles are guaranteed, in the hands of a good marksman, to be true at the same distance within eight inches. When his rifle was tested at Hythe with a Regulation Enfield, the efficiency of the one as compared with the other was as twenty to one: Colonel Wilford saying that the Whitworth was better at 800 yards than the Enfield at 500. Beyond 1100 yards the Enfield must cease firing even at large masses, while Whitworth's can do business at 2000. Indeed, rifling seems in its infancy, and range must only cease with the power of the human eye to take an aim. If Mr. Whitworth applies his peculiar principle of rifling to a breech-loader, he will produce the most finished weapon of the day.

Elliptical Firing. Mr. Lancaster's elliptical rifling gives excellent practice, and *the bore being smooth*, is not liable to harbour rust or wear away, and is easily cleaned.

Mr. Henry, of Edinburgh, has lately turned out most excellent arms of octagonal bore, the shooting of which can scarcely be surpassed, and the success they have won at the Wimbledon meeting has gained him a great name for careful workmanship.

Holster Pistols and Revolvers. For active service in the field, as well as for sporting purposes, I much prefer double-barrel breech-loading pistols for the holster to any revolver yet brought out, as it carries a very much larger bullet, which will disable even when it may not strike a vital part.

The sketch on the opposite page shows a holster pistol made by Westley Richards, which is all that can be desired.

For campaigning purposes abroad, when with

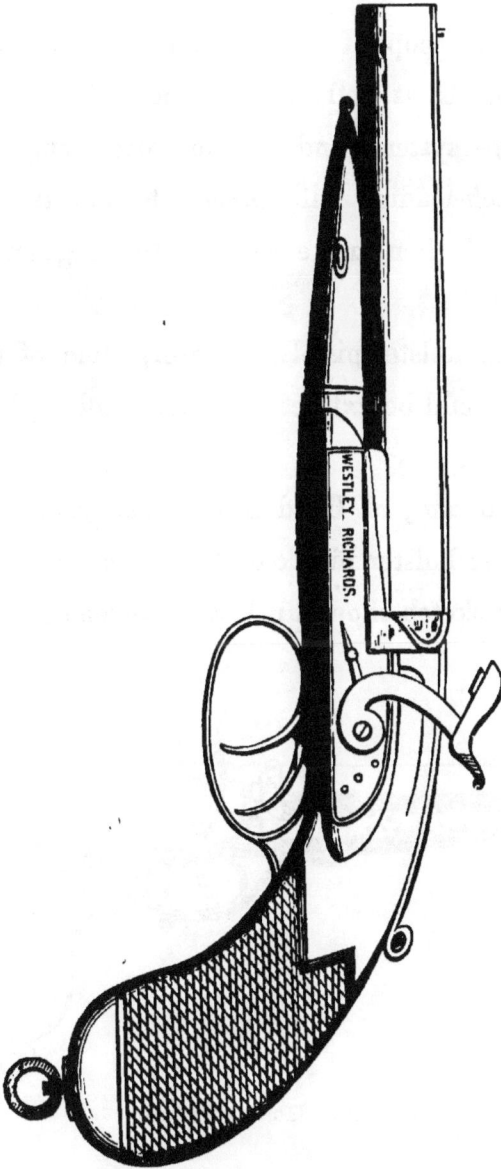

Westley Richards' Holster Pistol.

the regular troops, I should prefer to have my holster pistols, as well as my service rifle, on the central-fire system, and of the same gauge as the breech-loading rifle issued to the troops, as I could then make use of the regulation cartridges.

For the holster pistols, however, some of the powder should be extracted, or the recoil will be too great.

Mr. Holland, of Bond Street, has turned his attention to holster pistols on this system, and the following sketch shows his last improvements.

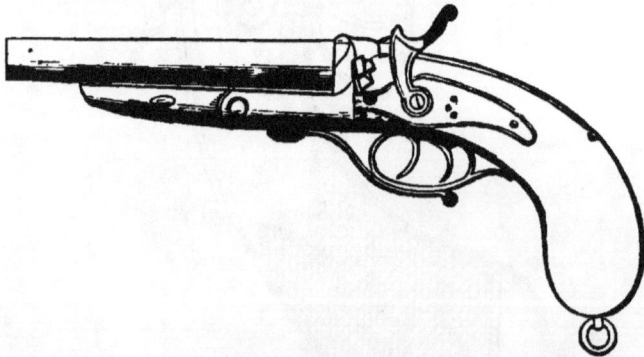

Holland's Holster Pistol.

Colt's Revolving Pistol.

1

For many years Colt's revolving arms have been considered to be the most efficient weapons of their kind for service in the field, having stood every test that practical experience can devise. In the Crimean, the late Continental, and the American wars, they have been very generally used, and have always proved to be most reliable and certain weapons.

For superiority

of material and workmanship, safety, simplicity, durability, accuracy, and celerity of fire, great length of range, force of penetration, they possess important advantages both for public and private service. The barrel is rifle-bored. The lever ramrod renders wadding or patch unnecessary, and secures the charge against moisture, or becoming loose by rough handling or hard riding. The hammer, when at full cock, forms the sight by which to take aim, and is readily raised to full cock by the thumb, with one hand.

A very effectual provision is made to prevent the accidental discharge of Colt's fire-arms whilst being carried in the hand, holster, pocket, or belt. Between each pair of nipples (the position of which secures the caps in their places) is a small pin or notch, and the point of the hammer is let down upon it; so that if the hammer be lowered on the pin, or into the notch, the cylinder is prevented from revolving, and the hammer is not in contact with the percussion cap, so that, even if the hammer be struck violently by accident, it cannot explode the cap.

Colt's Revolver,
with attachable
Carbine Breech.

The Carbine Breech attached to the 8-inch Barrel Army and Navy Revolver, Colt's latest improvement (*vide* Plate) is one by which the pistol may be made an efficient substitute for the carbines now in general use, without detracting from the special and peculiar qualities of the revolver. The weapon may be used with great facility and convenience as a carbine; and when not required for such use, the pistol may be removed and placed in the holster on the body, the butt or stock being allowed to swing from a strap or sling over the back, or at the side. An obvious advantage of this fitting is that, when in action, if all the charges of a repeating arm have been fired, the discharged pistol may be instantly exchanged for the other of the pair in the holster.

Directions.

Before loading blow the oil and dust out of the nipples.

Directions
for using
Colt's
Pistols.

Great care should be taken, when Colt's cartridges are not used, that all the balls are perfect, and fit the chambers snugly, otherwise the charges may jar out, and more than one chamber be discharged at once.

1st. Draw back the hammer to half-cock, which allows the cylinder to turn in one direction freely.

For Loading
and Firing.

2nd. Holding the muzzle erect, place a charge of powder in, and a ball upon the mouth of the chamber.

3rd. Turn the cylinder until the loaded chamber is under the rammer, and force the ball with the lever below the mouth of the chamber; if the ball fits, the chamber is then hermetically closed and the powder protected from water, damp, and sparks of fire.

4th. Reverse the arm and place the percussion caps on the nipples.

5th. Draw the hammer to full cock, and the arm is ready for firing.

For Cleaning. Set the hammer at half-cock, and drive out the key as far as the screw will allow, remove the barrel, which may be done by the aid of the lever pressing down the rammer upon the partitions between the chambers of the cylinder. Wash the cylinder and barrel in warm water, dry and oil them thoroughly, oil freely the base-pin on which the cylinder revolves, then replace the parts.

To take the Lock to Pieces, Clean and Oil. 1st. Set the hammer at half-cock, and drive ont the key or wedge which holds the barrel and cylinder to the lock frame, and remove the parts.

2nd. Turn out the bottom and two rear screws which fasten it to the trigger guard and lock frame, and remove the stock.

3rd. Loosen the screw that fastens the main spring to the guard, and turn the spring from under the hammer.

4th. Turn out the three screws which fasten the guard to the lock frame, and remove it.

5th. Turn out the screw, and remove the donble spring which bears upon the trigger and bolt.

6th. Turn out the side screws, and remove the trigger and bolt.

7th. Turn out the hammer screw, and remove the hammer with the hand attached, by drawing it downward out of the lock frame. Clean and oil all the parts thoroughly, and restore them to their places in the reverse order of separation.

Besides revolving pistols both for the belt and holster, which have been adopted by the British and the United States War Departments, carbines and rifles are also manufactured upon the same principle; which, in time of need, I have found to be most efficient weapons in every respect.

The Colt's Fire Arms Company, of 14, Pall Mall, are making experiments with a new breech-loading revolver, which, from all accounts, is a most efficient military weapon, likely to supersede all other systems, in which certain defects are known to exist, that have hitherto prevented European or American Governments from adopting any breech-loading revolver yet introduced.

Revolver Rifle.

Adams' Revolver.   This revolver has of late years been very generally adopted by officers in the Army and Navy, and in comparison with the old muzzle-loading pistol, it is a tolerably efficient arm, although far from being as good as is required for a service pistol.

It is unnecessarily heavy, carries too small a bullet, and cannot be depended upon for accuracy of shooting. This latter drawback is, however, chiefly occasioned by extreme carelessness in the manufacture, the barrels being irregularly bored, and the locks not properly regulated.

The patent having expired, these pistols are got up as cheaply as possible by small Birmingham houses, who make fire-arms wholesale, not to shoot, but. *to sell.*

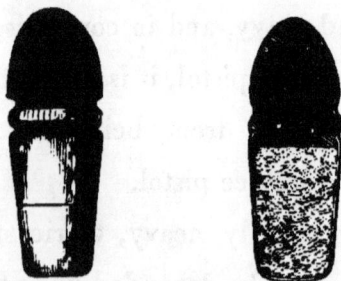

Revolver Skin Cartridge and Section.

Skin Cartridges.   This cartridge (*vide* Plate, above) the invention of Captain Montague Hayes, is the best for both Colt's and Dean's revolver, as the arm may be exposed to any weather without danger of the powder of the charge getting wet.

Revolver.   I prefer a breech-loading revolver on Tranter's system to any other yet brought out, as it is less complicated and handier to load, *although by no means perfect*, as it might be made much more serviceable if the barrel were shorter and the gauge very much larger.

The bullet carried by the present arm is much too small to be effective.

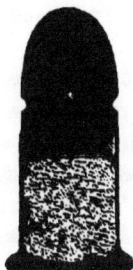

Section of Waterproof Copper Cartridge
for Tranter's Revolver.

Instructions for Loading. Raise the hammer till the trigger falls into the first bent, open the shield on the side, and put a cartridge in each hole of the chamber; close the shield, and the loading is complete. The cartridges can be withdrawn readily with the fingers, if not desired to be kept loaded. After the cartridges have been fired, the empty cases can be removed with the cleaning-rod. The pistol can be carried, when loaded, at "half-cock" for safety. The cartridges should be well covered with lubricating composition, before placing them in the chambers. The pistol should be well oiled after use.

Directions for Taking to Pieces and Putting Together. Remove the stock by taking out the two screws which fasten it to the frame, allowing the top strap to remain in the stock. Take off the main spring by placing the left thumb on the bent part, at the same time placing a turnscrew under the extremity of the short side, and gently lift it off the hook. Take out the two screws which hold the guard, and lift out the trigger-spring, which will then be loose. Take out the hammer-pin and the hammer, observing to press the lifting catch from the hammer with a small turnscrew. Take out the trigger pin, which will release the trigger and works attached to it. Take out the detent catch. Press down the lever catch, which will release the rod, and also the chamber; or the chamber may be removed first by pressing down the lever catch, and at the same time drawing the centre rod.

To put the revolver together again, clean and well oil every part. Put in the centre rod, then put in the chamber. Replace the detent catch, then the hammer, observing that the swivel is properly placed in it. Attach the claws of the main spring to the swivel; press down the main spring into its place on the hook with the fingers; affix the works to the trigger; replace it, taking care that the lifting catch is in front of the hammer. Replace the trigger-spring, screw on the guard and the stock.

"The Whisperer;" a rib-tickler.

"The Whisperer." This arm, which was built for me by Mr. H. Holland, of Bond Street, after my own design, is a rifle mounted on wheels, so as to be easily drawn by one man

over any kind of country with my wigwam
and ammunition. Taken to pieces, it all
packs on one mule. This "rib-tickler," as
a Yankee sportsman called it, was built for
me about three years ago for service in Central
Africa, and it is a most formidable arm either
against man or beast. It burns twelve drachms
of powder, and throws a cylindro-conical bullet
weighing half-a-pound, or a shell.

Breech-loading one- or two-pounder guns,
mounted on such carriages, would be very serviceable on service in the field, as those constructed by Mr. Whitworth, of Manchester, make
excellent practice with shot and shell at 2000
yards; and with a dozen of such pieces, I would
undertake to silence all the artillery of King
Theodore. They are superior to rockets, which
I class in the same category with "dollar" trade
guns made for the African market—as dangerous to the man who fires them as to the party
who is shot at. Their course is so erratic, and

their practice so uncertain, that, although they
may frighten savages, they rarely leave many
skins on the grass; in fact, their bark is much
worse than their bite.

CHAPTER V.

ARMAMENT.

Part III.—On the Selection of Arms.

Arms made *to Sell* and not to Shoot—Inferior Arms False Policy —On the Selection of Arms—First-class Arms the Cheapest in the End—Locks—The Testing of Guns and Rifles—The Proper Bend and Length of Stock—Confidence inspired by Good Arms.

"Caution."
Arms made to Sell.

For the present day, the market is deluged with arms that are made *to sell,* and not to shoot; and the public should be on their guard, so as not to allow themselves to be taken in by spurious imitations; for there are unscrupulous *vendors* who do not hesitate to engrave the names of first-class gunmakers upon guns of inferior workmanship, and sell them to the uninitiated as "bargains." Young sportsmen, in selecting a gun, should always go to a maker of note, who, for the sake of his own credit and reputation, would not allow an arm that is unsound, or of inferior workmanship, to leave his establishment bearing his name, which, in *first-class* work, *is always engraved in full, with address.* He may have to pay a long figure in comparison with the cost of the inferior article, and, perhaps, something for " the name ; " but he is sure of a good weapon, which will prove far better worth the money in the long run, and need not be apprehensive of accidents from defective workmanship or unsound material.

Inferior Arms.

Inferior guns, "made to sell," are now-a-days got up so well, that at first sight they resemble A 1 guns of best material and first-class workmanship; but the practical sportsman, on taking them in hand, soon discovers the counterfeit. There is no *music* in the locks; the strength of the mainsprings, as well as the *pull* of the triggers, is unequal; the barrels are imperfectly bored, or rough and unpolished in the interior, and perhaps the gauge shows that they are not of exactly the same calibre. Again, the lock-plate and mountings are not fitted and let in with that peculiar nicety that distinguishes first class London work; and the stock, in spite of a thick coat of French polish and varnish, betrays *greenness*, being made of unseasoned wood. I have seen some of these inferior guns throw shot pretty fairly to begin with, but, after a short time, they invariably fall off both in strength and regularity of shooting, become shaky, and even dangerous; for the locks (being made of soft metal, instead of the best tempered steel) begin to wear, and are no longer to be depended upon.

False Policy. It is mistaken policy and false economy to purchase any other than a first-class gun, which, with ordinary care, will last longer than half-a-dozen cheap ones of inferior workmanship, and give infinitely more satisfaction, to say nothing of the great additional security against accidents.

The following precautionary suggestions re-
lative to the choice and purchase of a gun, and
the best mode of trying its powers, may be of
service to the tyro.

If price be no object, the novice

On the
Selection of cannot do wrong by going to any
Fire-arms.

one of the half-dozen crack gun-
makers, Purday, Westley Richards, Lancaster,
Lang, or Boss, who will not compromise their
world-wide reputations by letting a bad gun
bearing their name leave their shops. By
naming these firms as first-rate artists in gun-
making, I by no means mean to infer that other
manufacturers are not practically as good, or as
much to be depended upon, as I know country
makers who turn out as highly finished work as
can be purchased in London. My object is to
disprove a doctrine often promulgated by the
ignorant, or interested parties attempting to im-
pose upon the credulity of the public, by the
unsound doctrine, "that cheaply made guns are
intrinsically as good, shoot as well, and last as

long as the highly-finished arms that command a high price." It is an egregious mistake. Cheaply got-up and roughly finished guns will invariably disappoint the purchaser, even if no worse result arises; and well-made, highly-finished guns always prove the cheapest in the end.

If money is an object, and the purchaser does not care to go to a long price, rather than allow himself to be deluded into buying an inferior article, let him go to one of the large London gun repositories such as Whistler's, in the Strand, where he can have the choice of several hundred second-hand guns and rifles by the best makers. Here anyone who is a judge of fire-arms can pick out as good and serviceable a gun as can be turned out, at about one-half its original cost.

Although sportsmen rarely care to part with really good arms, some people are whimsical, and like to change their guns as they do their coats; the consequence of which fancy is, that highly-finished guns that have hardly seen service are often in the market.

K

First-class Arms the Cheapest in the End.   A first-rate gun, made of the best materials, with all its component parts well fitted and finished, will last an ordinarily careful sportsman his lifetime. As a proof of this fact I may mention that I bought a 14-bore double gun, made by Westley Richards, from his agent, the Bishop of Bond Street, in 1843, with which I have shot so much that two pair of barrels were completely worn out, yet the locks and stock are as good as when first turned out of hand: I have also a Manton and a pair of Moore's that are known to be over thirty years old, yet are as serviceable as ever.

Old and well-seasoned walnut (the best wood for gun-stocks), never shrinks or gives way, the locks and barrels fitting as closely and well after twenty years' wear as they did in the first instance.

Locks.   Brazier's locks (which have been celebrated since the days of Manton) are so admirably made, the springs so carefully adjusted, and the steel so thoroughly tempered, that the friction after many years' use is scarcely productive of any appreciable or perceptible wear; so that they will generally survive two pairs of barrels, for barrels even of the best quality will give way and wear thin after much continuous shooting.

On the Selection of a Gun.

Let us suppose the purchaser, having selected half-a-dozen guns that appear to suit him as regards price, finish, length and bend of stock, bore, weight, etc., proceeds to the shooting ground, to test their capabilities of shooting, a proceeding I should always recommend (and which no respectable gunmaker will object to), before the purchase is concluded.

When ordering a new gun or rifle, I generally try the shooting whilst the gun is in the gray, before it is engraved and finished or the barrels browned, as when in this state the shooting can be altered with much less expense than when finished.

K 2

The Testing of Guns.   Nothing can be easier than to test the powers of a gun, which is the affair of a few minutes. Three things have to be considered, viz.: *the correctness of shooting; the penetration; and the regular distribution of the charge.*

The *correctness of shooting* is easily ascertained by firing at a small mark on the bull's eye of a target, and observing whether the barrels are so put together as to deliver the body of the charge fairly upon the point aimed at. If barrels are carelessly bored they often throw to the right or the left, high or low.

Guns also vary in throwing the charge, as more or less elevation is given to the muzzle of the barrels. In my opinion the elevated rib ought to be so regulated as to make the point-blank range forty or forty-five yards, as the generality of sportsmen oftener shoot under than over their game.

The best mode of testing *the penetration* of a gun is by firing at fifty sheets of brown paper, folded closely together, and fastened tightly on an iron target. A hard-hitting gun will drive No. 5 shot through forty sheets of ordinary brown cartridge paper at forty yards, thirty sheets at fifty yards, and twenty sheets at sixty yards. I have broken ordinary beer bottles at the latter distance with a favourite Joe Manton, but it was a gun among a thousand.

Having tested the penetration, the next thing is to ascertain if the gun *distributes the charge regularly*, and this a few shots at a large white-washed iron target will soon determine. The shots ought to strike very close and regular in the middle, gradually spreading as they diverge from the centre.

When no paper is at hand, some idea may be formed as to the penetrating powers of the gun by observing the state of the shot that has re-coiled from the target. It is flattened in pro-portion to the force with which the gun shoots.

The elevation and regularity of the distri-bution of the charge is also shown by firing at

water on a still day, when the surface is smooth
and unruffled.

It is not sufficient that a gun is well
The Bend and
Length of   finished and hard hitting, it must suit
Stock.
the sportsman in the length and bend
of the stock, so that *it comes up at once well* to
the shoulder, and strikes the object aimed at with
the first motion.   This enables the hand and eye
to act simultaneously, the great desideratum necessary for good and quick shooting.   No one
can shoot brilliantly with a gun that does not
come up well.   .A gun should be built according
to the length of arm and neck of the sportsman ;
for, in many cases men can no more use the same
gun than they can wear each other's coats.

A well-finished good gun gives con-
Good Arms
inspire Confi- fidence to the sportsman, whereas an
dence,Inferior
Ones Disgust.   inferior one destroys it, besides being
productive of bad shooting.   There is no reason
why anyone should not shoot well who has tolerable eyesight, and begins early in life, but there
are certain requisites a gun must have, or the best

performer will make but a sorry bag. Let the
sportsman exercise his best judgment in choosing
his gun, and remember that the purchase of an
inferior article is not only false economy, but
great imprudence, if he sets any value on his
personal safety.

CHAPTER VI.

PRACTICAL HINTS ON THE USE OF THE RIFLE.

The Theory of Rifle Practice—The Rifle, the Bullet, the Line of Fire, the Trajectory, Point Blank Range—The Line of Sight —Sights—Aiming Drill—Position Drill—Two Steady Positions for Long Range Practice—Blank Cartridge Firing— Judging Distance Drill—Target Practice—Hints upon Loading : Allowances to be made for the Wind, the State of the Atmosphere, and the Position of the Sun—Rules to be observed when Firing at Moving Objects.

THE following hints on rifle-shooting may prove useful to those who have not had the benefit of an efficient instructor.

Riflemen are not made in a day, but it is an established fact that anyone gifted with perfect vision can, with *instruction* and *practice*, become an efficient marksman; therefore, none should be discouraged or despair, as *perseverance must lead to ultimate success.*

Commencing with the *theory* of rifle practice, which must be fully understood before the rifleman can hope to be an expert shot at all ranges, I shall afterwards enter upon the *practical* part of his initiation.

The Rifling. The first point for consideration is the barrel of the rifle, which (in the Enfield pattern), it may be observed, has three spiral grooves cut in the interior, or *bore,* at an equal distance from each other, of even depth, and making half a turn in the length of the barrel, which is 3 feet 3 inches. These grooves, otherwise termed the *rifling,* give the bullet (an elongated cylindro-conical projectile) a spiral motion, sometimes called the *spin* or *twist,* as it flies through the air point foremost, rotatory on its own axis. This very much increases the accuracy of the flight of the bullet, as it serves to keep it in its true course, and prevents any inclination it may have to deviate from it, owing to irregularity in shape or weight.

Windage.

The diameter of the bore of an Enfield rifle is ·577, but that of the bullet is rather less, in order to facilitate the loading. This difference in size—*i.e.*, the difference between the circumference of the bullet and the bore—leaves a space between the bullet and the bore, termed the *windage*, which was the principal cause of the inefficiency of the old " Brown Bess," for two reasons—the first, because a great part of the explosive force, or gas generated by the ignition of the powder, was lost, as it escaped by the space between the bullet and the side of the bore; and, secondly, because this irregular escape caused the ball to rebound from side to side in the barrel, instead of passing evenly through the bore, and the consequence of this was that it took an erratic impetus throughout its flight.

The Bullet. The Enfield bullet is, however, so constructed as to do away with these objections. Although the circumference is much less than that of the bore, so as to enter the barrel easily in loading, *all windage is effectually prevented*, as in the base of the projectile is a hollow, into which is fitted a small wooden *cup*, or *plug* (*vide* Plate), which, by the force of the explosion of the charge, acts like a wedge,* and expands and enlarges the lower part of the bullet, making it fit the barrel

SECTION OF THE ENFIELD CARTRIDGE. tightly, and *take the rifling*, so that in its passage through the barrel it is constrained to turn with the grooves, and thus receives the spinning movement on its longer axis, which not only insures accuracy of flight,

---

* This theory, although adopted by the School of Musketry at Hythe, is contradicted by several competent authorities; and I believe there is reason to doubt its accuracy.

but also always keeps its point forward. By the
bullet being thus expanded, and so much enlarged as to fit the barrel and grooves tightly,
none of the explosive power of the gas engendered by the ignition of the charge is allowed to
escape, but the whole propelling force acts
upon the projectile. There is also a much
better chance of the whole of the powder being
burnt.

The Barrel. The barrel is a tube of iron, of
which the sides of the interior, or
bore, are parallel, but those of the exterior converge, it being necessary that the metal of the
breech-end should be very much thicker than at
the muzzle, towards which it gradually tapers,
as it has to stand the force of the explosion of
the charge. In consequence of this contraction,
every barrel has in itself a certain degree of
elevation—but of this more anon.

The Axis. The *axis* of the barrel is an imaginary line drawn through the centre of
the bore, and parallel to the interior sides.

The *line of fire* is the continuation of the axis in a straight line, and marks the direction the bullet would take on leaving the barrel, *propelled by the explosion* of the charge, were it not that it is also acted upon by the *power of gravity*, which attracts it towards the earth, and the *resistance the air offers to its passage,* which is always in direct opposition to its flight.

The *trajectory* is the actual course of the bullet, *which dalways escribes a curve*—a fact easily accounted for, as, from the moment it leaves the muzzle, the force of the gunpowder drives it forward, and gravity draws it downward, so that by yielding to both forces— *i.e.*, by moving onwards and downwards at the same time—it must travel in a curve diverging more and more below the line of fire, until at last, the propelling power being expended, it falls to the earth. Hence it follows, that if the axis of a barrel is directed upon the bull's-eye of a target, at 100 yards distance, the bullet will

strike about 1 foot 5 inches below; the power
of gravity having made it deviate from the
line of fire, and drawn it towards the earth, 1 foot
and 5 inches, in a flight of 100 yards. Therefore,
if the barrel were as thick at the muzzle as it is at
the breech, it would be necessary to aim 1 foot
5 inches above the mark in order to hit it; but
this is not the case, for, as I have before observed,
every barrel has in itself a certain degree of
elevation, on account of the increased thickness of metal at the breech end. The Enfield
rifle-barrel has elevation in itself for about 75
yards.

Point-blank
Range.
      The point-blank range is the extreme
point at which the trajectory intersects
the line of fire, or the greatest distance to which
a rifle will throw a ball in a direct course parallel
to the line of sight.

If an Enfield rifle be held with the axis of the
barrel parallel to the ground at the height of
4 feet 6 inches above it, the first graze when the
bullet strikes will be about 200 paces distant,

the ball having dropped 4½ feet in that distance. The point-blank range of an Enfield is about 80 paces; but they vary, as more or less elevation is given to the muzzle of the rifle, or according to the strength of the propelling power.

Line of Sight.

The *line of sight*, or aim, is an imaginary straight line taken from the pupil of the eye through the centre of the back-sight, along the top of the fore-sight, to the object intended to be hit. The back-sight is so arranged as to give the proper elevation for different distances. The further the object is to be aimed at, the greater the elevation required; and this is given by raising the sliding bar of the back-sight, which is marked with lines up to 900 yards.

Sights.

Accuracy of shooting is greatly dependent upon the sights being carefully adjusted, and fitted exactly parallel to the axis of the barrel. If the back-sight is too much inclined to the right, or the front-sight too much to the left, the rifle will shoot to the right of the mark aimed at; in the same manner, if the back-sight is placed too much to the left, or the fore-sight too much to the right, the gun will carry to the left; and the greater the distance the greater in proportion will be the deviation. Every rifle, therefore, ought to be carefully sighted and shot before it is placed in a novice's hands, as non-success in practice on account of an ill-sighted weapon would not be his fault, and might serve to discourage him.

The Routine of Drill.

The mechanical routine necessary to be gone through before the tyro can become an efficient marksman, consists of *aiming drill, position drill, judging distance drill,* and *practice in firing.*

Aiming Drill.

AIMING DRILL is necessary to familiarise the uninitiated with the use of the sights, teaching him how to *align* his rifle, or *aim* correctly at a mark. The practice of this drill exercises the eye, strengthening and developing the sight in the same manner that continued exertion increases the power of the limbs. The following standard rules should be carefully observed:

I.—*The rifle should always be held with the sights perfectly upright*, as it is only in this position that the *line of sight*, the *line of fire*, and *trajectory*, are in the same vertical plane. If the butt of the rifle is not held *vertically*, but is "canted" either to the right or the left, so that *the perpendicular of the back-sight with the axis* of the barrel is not preserved, the ball will strike to the right if the sight inclines to the left, and *vice versâ;* and, in firing at long ranges, a very slight deviation in this respect will cause a wide deflection.

II.—The *aim* or *line of sight* should be taken along the centre of the notch of the back-sight and the top of the fore-sight, which should cover the centre of the object aimed at.

III.—The eye should be fixed *steadfastly* on the mark aimed at, and not on the barrel or fore-sight, which latter will be easily brought into the alignment, if the eye is fixed as directed.

IV.—In aiming, the left eye should be closed.
Aiming drill is generally taught with a " traver-
sing rest," or, if that is not at hand, a tripod
with a sand-bag on the top, standing about
4 feet 8 inches from the ground (or the average
height of a man's shoulder) will answer every
purpose ; and the novice is required to align his
rifle with the proper elevation upon objects at
distances varying from 50 to 900 yards. Each
time he has aligned his rifle he steps aside,
in order that the instructor may take his
place and see if the aim be correct. This practice should be continued until the novice has no
difficulty in aligning his rifle on the bull's eye at
all distances. Up to 300 yards, the bull's eye is
8 inches in diameter, and above that distance
2 feet.

POSITION DRILL is absolutely ne-
Position Drill.
cessary to insure good practice at
long ranges. It *habituates* the novice to correct positions, and enables him to fire steadily in
all situations. It gives him a perfect command

over his weapon, and enables the eye and hand to act together, so that the left hand raises the rifle at once to bear upon the object, for the eye to take aim; and at the same moment the forefinger of the right hand acts upon the trigger.

To establish the natural connection between the eye and the hand, constant practice is required; and the novice should be accustomed to handle his rifle *both with and without the bayonet*, being put through all the motions of firing *standing and kneeling*, with the same precision as if actually practising with ball-cartridge.

At the School of Musketry at Hythe, recruits are taught to fire *standing* at all distances up to 300 yards, and *kneeling* at every longer range.

There are *two* positions for taking a steady aim without artificial appliance :

Kneeling Position. The first is by kneeling on the right knee and sitting on the right heel, the rifle being firmly grasped and steadied by the left hand, the left elbow resting on the left knee. so as to form a support.

Sitting
Position.

The second is by sitting on the ground with both feet fairly planted flat, and the knees raised so as almost to form a right-angle. The left elbow rests on the left knee, which is pointed in the direction of the object aimed at, and the right elbow rests on the right knee, which is extended to the right.

The latter, in my opinion, is *the firmest* position the marksman can adopt in shooting at long ranges, and after a little practice it becomes a very comfortable one.

Lying down.

In practising at long ranges, or when exposed to heavy fire, the marksman can make very good shooting by lying down his full length upon his belly, and firing with his head slightly raised, and with his two elbows resting steadily on the ground.

Snapping
aps.

Should the novice meet with any difficulty in aiming correctly, the inspector should cause him to snap caps at a lighted candle placed about a yard distant, when, if the aim is properly directed, the candle will be extinguished. The novice should be attentively watched during this practice, until all tendency to wink or flinch is overcome, and his countenance shows that he has become indifferent to the report.

This practice is *most excellent* for forming "*Marksmen*," for, besides saving ammunition, it may be continually resorted to, even in a room, the bulls'-eye being a small black wafer on the wall at one end, and the stand taken at the other. By snapping caps only, the young beginner is enabled to see whether the muzzle of the barrel wavers when he presses the trigger, which he cannot properly ascertain when firing ball, on account of the smoke of the discharge. The constant handling of the rifle in a proper manner, by aiming at various objects at different distances, enables the "finger to work in unison with the eye," and gives great steadiness of position before, during, and after pressing the trigger, which is all that is required in making good ball-practice at a target of which the distance is known.

Blank
Cartridge.
Before the novice is allowed to fire with ball, he should practise a certain routine of blank-cartridge firing, in order to further the same object for which he was exercised in snapping caps, as well as to accustom him to the "*recoil*" or "kick," which is a backward motion caused by the force of the explosion of the powder acting against the breech of the barrel at the same time as against the bullet.

Recoil.
The *force of the recoil* depends upon *the charge* of powder, the weight of the bullet, the weight of the rifle, the windage, the rifling of the barrel, the boring of the barrel (whether purely cylindrical or otherwise), the amount of friction, and the foulness, which much increases the resistance offered by the air to the bullet passing up the barrel. The instructor should impress upon the novice the necessity of pressing the heel of the butt well and firmly into the hollow of the shoulder, as the more confidently a man "stands up" to his rifle, the less likelihood there is of random shooting.

The position of the body, arms, and hands, and the manner of pressing the trigger, as also the position of the head when taking aim, are to be duly watched both in this and the former exercise, in order to discover and correct those errors which are fatal to good shooting, and which cannot be so successfully corrected when firing ball.

Judging Distance. One of the greatest essentials in a well-trained marksman is the capability to estimate distances correctly, as good shooting cannot be made unless the distance is previously ascertained and the proper elevation given to the back-sight. At long ranges it requires great practice to judge distance accurately; but there is always a ready method of ascertaining it practically, by firing, and watching whether the bullet strikes the ground over or under the object aimed at. If over, he will lower the sliding bar of the back-sight; if under, he will raise it. Practice over all kinds of ground is the best means of teaching a novice how to judge distance correctly by the eye, and anyone possessing good vision may train himself most effectually in this art for all practical purposes. This, however, can only be accomplished by continual practice and careful observation. When engaged in ball-practice at a target placed at known distances, the tyro should carefully notice the *apparent* height of the markers at each range, remembering that in fine clear weather objects standing in a strong light will appear much nearer than they really are, and *vice versâ* in cloudy and damp weather.

Rule. At 50 yards, the features of a man may be clearly identified, and his complexion, arms, accoutrements, and dress distinctly perceived, the buttons and the badge on his forage-cap being distinguishable. At 100 yards, the features become indistinct, the buttons appear in a line, and the badge can be only faintly discerned. At 200 yards, the face appears like a whitish ball under the line of the cap, and the buttons and badge become invisible.

These distances should constitute the first practice; the second would embrace distances from 200 to 400 yards; and the third, from 400 to 1000 yards or more. At 500 yards no features are visible, and the head looks like a ball upon the shoulders, the neck being hardly visible.

The instructor will desire the novice to mark the size of the men at each distance, and point out any difference he may discern in their appearance. He will also desire him to take notice of the position of the sun, the character of the background, and state of the atmosphere at the time, in order that he may be accustomed to their altered appearance under different circumstances.

After some days' exercise in Judging Distance Drill, the proficiency of the novice may be tested by his being practised to judge the distance of objects placed at unknown ranges.

Target Practice. The novice having been thoroughly instructed in " *aiming*," "*position*," and "*judging distance*" drill, can commence "*target practice,*" when his efficiency will be tested.

The following hints may prove useful to the novice:

At the moment of *pressing* the trigger, the act of respiration should be suspended, to ensure greater steadiness of aim.

When once the aim is clearly taken, all delay in pressing the trigger is prejudicial to good shooting; as, if the rifle is held at the " present " too long, a " *wavering* " of the muzzle takes place, and an uncertain shot is the consequence.

Taking Aim.   In taking aim at a target, fix the eye steadfastly on the bull's eye, grasping he rifle *firmly with the left hand* " well forward " (according to its balance), the butt being *pressed home* into the hollow of the shoulder; the right hand, with the exception of the forefinger, *lightly* clasping the small of the stock behind the trigger-guard, so as to steady and preserve the butt in a vertical position; then, holding the breath, place the fore finger well round the trigger, feeling it

lightly, and raise the muzzle gradually and
steadily until the fore-sight is seen through the
centre of the notch of the back-sight covering the
centre of the bull's-eye, when the motion should
be arrested, and the trigger simultaneously pressed
without the slightest jerk, the eye being rigidly
fixed on the object aimed at, and the whole of the
body *immobile*.

On the Hand
and Eye work-
ing together.
The great " knack " in rifle-practice
is to accustom *the hand and eye to
work together,* so that the trigger be
pressed simultaneously with the object being
" covered," as it is almost an impossibility to
retain an aim.

Care should be taken that the aim is not lost in
pressing the trigger, which, if the lock is well
made, should not "pull too strongly."

After the trigger is pressed—keeping the rifle
to the shoulder—a perfect immobility of body
should be retained, and the eye kept steadfastly
upon the object aimed at, and the deflection
noted.

In aligning a rifle at a mark, the position of the head with reference to the butt will vary according to the range and the elevation required. At short distances, the shoulder is a little raised and the head bent forward (not sideways), the cheek resting against the small part of the butt, so that the object aimed at is seen through the notch in the back-sight. At longer ranges, the head must be raised, and the shoulder lowered; and at the furthest distances, if the stock of the rifle is too much bent, the heel of the butt may rest against the breast or side instead of the shoulder. As heavy firing in this position is inconvenient, it is perhaps better in this case to allow for the necessary elevation by *firing high,* or aiming above the object intended to be hit, as the recoil is often felt severely when the heel of the butt only rests against the shoulder.

Careless
Loading.
Careless loading is conducive to irregular firing. The exact charge of powder that the rifle will burn should be correctly ascertained and strictly adhered to, for a

little more or a little less will cause a great vertical deviation in the flight of the bullet. Care should be taken to keep the barrel upright when pouring in the charge, so that the grains of powder may not adhere to the sides of the barrel, which would foul and impede the passage of the bullet.

The bullet should not fit too *loosely* nor yet be so large as to require hammering, in order to force it down, as in the former case it is liable "to strip" (or pass out of the barrel without taking the rifling, and gaining the spiral motion), and in the latter it will have ragged edges, which will cause it to diverge from its true direction in its flight through the air.

In *pressing* down the bullet, although great care should be taken to drive it properly *home*, much force should not be employed, as, by *ramming* and *jamming* with the ramrod, the shape of the bullet is altered and spoiled, which much affects its true flight, and the powder is "mealed" and "caked," by which the strength of the charge in much diminished, as a certain amount

of air is necessary to ensure thorough com-
bustion.

The base of the bullet should rest evenly upon
the powder, and its axis be in line with that of
the barrel.

For fine shooting, care should be taken that
there is no hidden defect in the bullet, for if any
part be hollow or imperfect, the centre of gravity
will not be in the line of the axis, and consequently there will be a deviation in its flight.

I shall now notice the causes of irregular firing
over which the rifleman can have no control, but
which may, to a certain extent, be rendered less
injurious to " the score " if the following observations are carefully attended to :

Allowance for
Wind.
First, *the wind* affects the flight of
the bullet to a considerable extent in
firing at long distances, diverting it from its true
course, and accelerating or retarding its progress
according as it blows *with* or *against* it. When
the wind blows from a quarter exactly *opposite*
to the direction of the bullet, it experiences a

greater resistance in its flight, and accordingly more *elevation* should be given. Should the wind blow exactly from the shooter to the target the resistance will be *less* than ordinary, and consequently *less* elevation than ordinary is required. Allowances should be made according to the strength of the current of air. If the wind blows from the *right*, aim to the *right*, as the deflection will be to the *left*, and *vice vers* if from the *left*.

If the course of the wind *forms an angle* to the direction of the bullet, aim must be taken, and allowances made accordingly. Thus, if the wind blows from the *right* and *contrary*, the deviation will be to the *left* and *low:* therefore, in order to strike the bull's-eye, aim should be taken to the *right* and *high;* and to the *left* and *high* if the current of air is *contrary*, and from the left.

If the wind blows from the *right* and *rear*, on aiming direct at the bull's-eye, the deflection of the bullet will be to the *left* and *high:* therefore, in such a case, aim should be taken to the *right* and *low ;* or to the *left* and *low*, if the current of air comes from the *left* and *rear*.

Correct judgment in making the proper allowances for the effect of various winds upon the flight of the projectile can only be gained by practice in all kinds of weather, but the above hints may assist the novice.

State of the Atmosphere. The *state of the atmosphere* considerably affects the *range* of the bullet. In damp weather, when the atmosphere is dense, its resistance to the flight of the bullet is *increased*, and consequently *greater elevation* should be given. In fine clear weather, on the contrary, the resistance is *less*, and the bullet *rises*, therefore *less* elevation is required. Humidity in the atmosphere also affects the range of the bullet in a different manner, as it has a certain influence on ignition of gunpowder, which in damp weather is not so rapid as in fine ; therefore, on such days larger charges should be used than on hot summer days.

Position of
the Sun.
The *position of the sun* is sometimes liable to influence the correct
aim, as if it shines from the *right* it lightens up
the *right* side of the front-sight, and the *left* side
of the notch of the back-sight, throwing the *left*
of the front-sight and the *right* of the back-sight
into the shade; therefore, if the firer is not careful in aiming properly, the "line of sight" is
liable to pass from the *left* of the centre of the
notch of the back-sight and the *right* of the front-
sight, the effect of which would be that the bullet
would strike to the *left*, and *vice versâ* if the sun
shines from the *left*. Sun-shades are sometimes
used to obviate this difficulty.

Allowance
for Moving
Objects.
It must be obvious to all, that the
flight of the bullet occupies a certain
time, and in firing at *moving* objects a certain
allowance should be made accordingly, and great
judgment is required in this point when firing
at long ranges. For instance, in deer-stalking,
if a deer is running *transversely* either to the
right or left, a sportsman aiming directly at the

M

shoulder would most likely either strike the hind-quarter or miss by shooting behind, as, in the time between the *discharge* of his rifle and the *impact* or striking of the bullet, the quarry would have moved forward a certain distance.

The following hints on this point may aid the novice:

In firing at anything moving, it is advisable to *cover* the object and allow the muzzle to follow it for some distance before pulling the trigger, in order to ascertain the velocity of the motion, and the allowance required to be made.

If the object is *approaching* the person firing, the muzzle of the barrel should be gradually *lowered,* the finger feeling the trigger all the time, and aim should be taken *low.*

If the object be *retiring,* the muzzle of the rifle should be raised (more or less according to the distance and the velocity of motion of the object), and aim taken *high.*

If the object is moving across, either to the

right or left, aim should be taken *well forward,* after having followed the motion with the object well covered for some time.

Should the object be *ascending* a hill, *fire high;* if *descending, fire low;* if *diagonally, in front.*

CHAPTER VII.

TENTS AND ENCAMPMENTS.

I SHALL now enter upon the subject of *tents,* for
much of a traveller's comfort depends upon his
having a commodious shelter impervious to wind
or weather, sufficiently portable *to be always carried with him,* which, unfortunately for our poor
soldiers, Government tents are not. Many a
thousand brave fellows have been laid under the

Tents and Encampments.

sod, wasted away from disease contracted on service, because, when weary at the end of a long
march, their tents not having come up, they have
thrown themselves upon the damp ground, or
slept exposed to the deadly night-dews. After
the intense heat of the day, a night passed in this
manner will undermine the strongest constitution,

and lay in the seeds of rheumatism, fever, and dysentery.

The following sketches show the different kinds of tents in general use, all of which are to be obtained at B. Edgington's establishment, in Duke Street, near London Bridge, which firm for many years has borne the palm for all kinds of camp equipment

Regulation Bell Tent.

The above Plate shows the Regulation Bell

Tent, which has a circumference of 40 feet, and is supposed to hold a dozen men.

Officers' Bell Tent.

The above Plate shows an Officers' Tent, which is a modification of the soldiers', having low side walls, and standing on the same area.

Round Wall Tent.

The above Plate shows a Round Wall Tent,
much used in India and other hot climates, being
more convenient, but at the same time considerably heavier, than the regulation tents. It is also
much more liable to be blown down.

The Plate on page 169 shows the Marquee of an
officer commanding a regiment, or an Indian Mess
Tent. It makes a great show in a camp, and is
very spacious and comfortable dining in, but
sometimes comes to grief in a storm.

An Indian Mess Tent, or Marquee.

Regulation Tent of the French Army.

The Plate on page 170 shows the tent much used by the French army during the campaign in the Crimea. In fine weather it is far more commodious than the English Regulation Bell Tent, but it is not so comfortable in wet weather, and is considerably heavier, weighing 160 lbs. It makes a very nice tent for a pic-nic, or for a lawn.

Shooting Tent.

The Plate on page 171 shows a very convenient little tent for shooting on the moors, but it will not stand heavy weather. It holds two persons very comfortably.

The two Plates, pages 173 and 174, show B. Edgington's Military Tent, which is superior in every respect to that now in use in the British army. It is 14 feet

B. Edgington's Improved Military Tent.

6 inches square, with porches at each end projecting 6 feet, and sustained by light 6-feet poles, protecting the entrance from rain. The figure is a pyramid, and the angles are strengthened from the head of the tent by an inch rope, to which the canvas is bolted, and which, being secured by strong iron pegs to the ground, constitutes the principal support of the tent. "The ventilation" is at the top, the aperture being secured against the entrance of rain. The centre pole is divided into three parts—the small poles into two, and the whole (including poles, pegs, and every requisite) is packed in two

B. Edgington's Improved Military Tent.

B. Edgington's Improved Military Tent, showing the Interior.

valises ; weight of tent, 93 lbs. and 79 lbs. poles, etc. Area of tent with porches, 394 square feet. This tent is also made 9 and 11 feet square.

For cold weather a stove and chimney can be substituted for a centre-pole, and by means of a rack, the top of the tent can be raised or lowered, according to the action of the weather on the canvas, the pipe being free from the stove. The Plate on page 174 shows the arrangement of the stove.

"The Old Shekarry's Wigwam."

I herewith give a sketch of a very comfortable tent of my own invention, which I have found very serviceable when a small amount of baggage only can be taken. It is water-tight, weather-proof, well ventilated, and very portable.

The dimensions are :

Length of top ridge, *a* to *b*, 10 feet.

Slope, 7 feet.

Height of poles, 5 feet, to lengthen to 7 feet.

"The Old Shekarry's Wigwm."

The Interior of "The Old Shekarry's Wigwam."

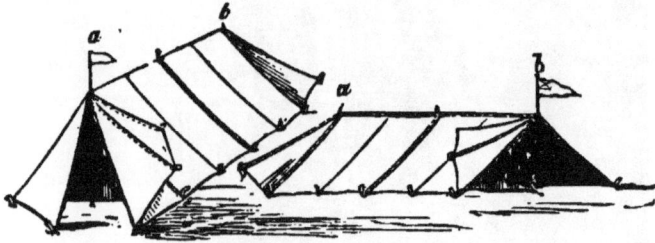

"The Wigwam."

This tent or wigwam, as I term it, is very comfortable for two persons, with their baggage, and, if required, four can find ample room in it to sleep.   Although a man cannot stand upright in my tent (the height being only 5 feet in the centre), without digging out the inside area—as in my expeditions I rarely travel with table, chair, or even bedstead—I suffer very little inconvenience from the low pitch; and, on the other hand, I go to sleep with the comfortable assurance in my mind that, although the winds may blow and the rains descend, my home is impervious to both. Mr. Benjamin Edgington, of Duke Street, Southwark, has built me a famous wigwam for Abyssinia, which has all the edges strongly roped, so that it will stand the brunt of any storm.

When only one tent is taken, and the journey is likely to be a long one, perhaps it would be advisable to have a somewhat larger wigwam. Mr. Edgington is building some 8 feet in height, and 8 feet broad, in which there is plenty of room for a stove, the chimney forming a substitute for the centre-pole.

The Plate on page 177 shows the interior of the larger "wigwam," with the interior dug out, which, including the porches, has an area of about 18 feet by 8, and is a very comfortable habitation for four officers in any weather.

"The wigwam," having two entrances opposite each other (which are protected from the weather by the porches), the ventilation can be regulated at will ; a thorough current of air always passing through the tent, which is a *great desideratum* in a hot climate.

With every " wigwam," Mr. Edgington sends out an extra piece, with an iron socket attached, to lengthen the centre-pole, when the inside area is dug out, also storm ropes in case of hurricanes, and a canvas saddle-bag, which contains the whole tent.

The wigwam, having no outlying ropes, stands on a smaller area of ground than most other descriptions of tent, and can therefore be pitched close to another, with only a centre drain between them.   This is a great advantage when a large force is encamped, and the ground is circumscribed.

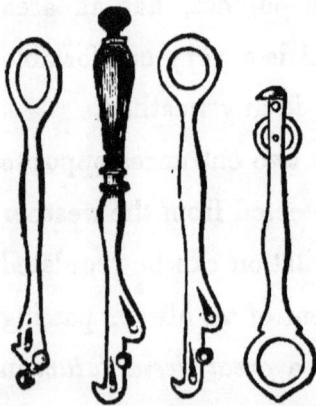

Tent Pegs.

I prefer galvanised iron tent-pegs to wooden ones.   They should have a notch to hold the rope, and rings passing through the ends to sling them together, and prevent their being lost when on the march.

How to Pitch a Tent.   Great art is shown in pitching a tent properly, so as to stand firmly with the canvas tightly stretched.   Care must be taken to dig a trench outside, to carry away the rain-water (*vide* Plate, page 177, *b*); and to raise a bank of earth in the inside (*vide* Plate, page 177, *a*), to prevent wind, dust, or draught from coming in under the canvas sides. When it is intended to remain for any length of time in a place, the interior area of the tent may be excavated, leaving a shelf of about 18 inches in width all round; and the centre pole being lengthened or the stove set up, it then becomes a most commodious habitation.

In case of bad weather, storm-ropes should be fastened to the spokes of the tent-poles and pegged securely, taking care that the tent-pegs are driven in a sloping direction, inclining inwards, so that they are less easily drawn out.

Should the soil be sandy, the ropes ought to be *bushed,* which is done by burying branches deeply, and only leaving a hook above the surface, to which the rope is attached (*vide* Plate, page 180). Two tent-pegs may be buried in a similar manner but the former arrangement holds best in a light soil.

Edgington's Camp Stove and Cooking Apparatus. This arrangement (Plate, page 183), which is particularly well adapted for tents, is remarkable alike for its utility and compactness. The whole packs into an oval case (12), 22 inches high, 16 inches long, and 13 inches wide. Weight, 80 lbs.

The following articles are contained : Camp stove (1); two-gallon boiling pot (2), the cover of which forms a frying pan (3); one-gallon tea kettle with swing handle and screw spout (4); two one-quart hooked coffee boilers (5); four oval bottles for essence of coffee, etc. (6); one meat dish (7); one soup ditto (8); one toasting oven (9); oval box and pepper box (10); one pint porringer (11).

Directions for Use. Place the stove in the oval pan, which forms the cover of the iron box; fix the circular rim on the top of the stove, on which place the boiler, frying pan, or tea kettle, as required.

Camp Stove and Cooking Apparatus.

The hooked pots will hang on the sides or front of the stove. When not required for cooking, put on the round cast top; the large oval box will hold the fuel.

Directions for Packing. The articles to be put into the stove in the following order: 1st—Deep dish and toasting oven. 2nd—Meat dish. 3rd—Frying pan. 4th—Boiling pot, in which place the two hooked pots, oval boxes, and pepper box. (The oval bottles will go into the hooked pots.) 5th—The tea kettle, in which place the porringer. 6th—The stove, funnel pipes, and elbows to be placed within the case. The oval pan forms the cover.

On the opposite page is an engraving of a very compact and useful little dinner apparatus; knife, fork, and spoon, each closing up like a pocket-knife, and fitting, with salt, pepper, and mustard-pots, into a leather case, which, when rolled up, is contained in the drinking-cup. The whole fits into a compact leather case, which can be strapped to the saddle.

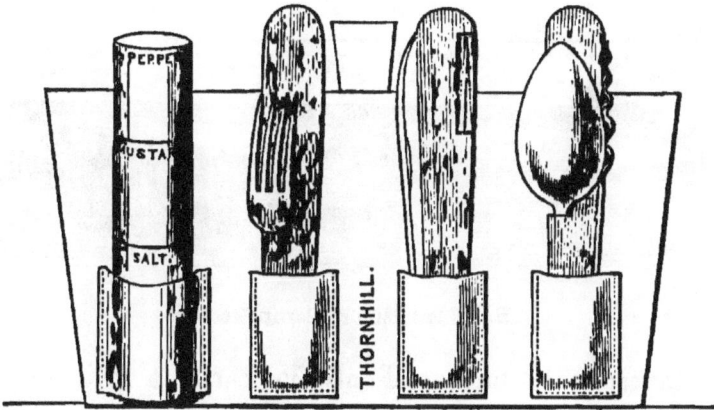

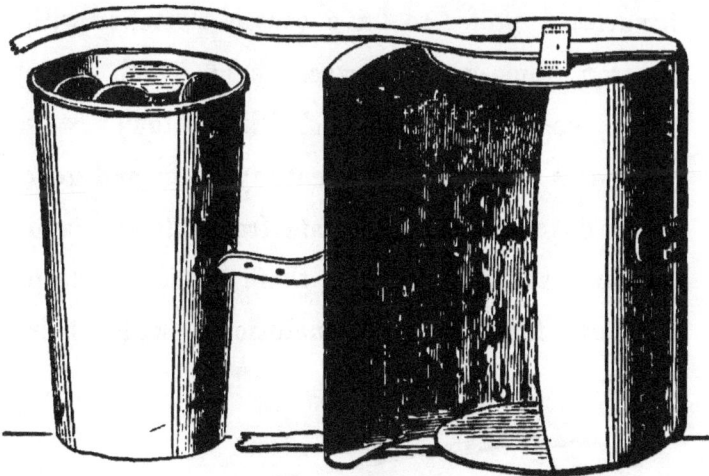

Dinner Apparatus.

Tent
Furniture.
A portable bedstead, as made by
B. Edgington, of 2, Duke Street, Lon-
don Bridge (*vide* Plate, page 186). is not a bad

B. Edgington's Camp-Bed.

investment, but as I always carry a pair of
bullock trunks when I intend to indulge in
luxuries, I prefer to fix a canvas stretcher with
an iron frame-work between them, which forms
a very comfortable bed (*vide* Plate below).

By this latter arrangement my goods and gear
in the boxes are tolerably safe from pilferers, and
no one can meddle with them whilst I sleep
without first trying conclusions with their
owner.

Bengough's Trunk-Bed.

Cording's Inflatable Bath.

A portable bath is a great luxury, and those of india-rubber, inflated with air, made by Cording, 231, Strand, are by far the best I have seen.

The Hammock. When the inside area of the tent is excavated, it is an easy matter to sling a hammock to ropes fixed to tent-pegs or posts firmly driven into the ground, and in my opinion this makes the most comfortable bed. I always carry one of Cording's waterproof hammocks with me, which, even if I cannot sling it, serves me as a ground-sheet.

Slung from a bamboo or pole, it makes a capital stretcher for a sick or wounded man; on the West Coast of Equatorial Africa, where horses will not live, it is the only mode of conveyance for Europeans, in getting about from place to place.

In Madeira, South America, and throughout India, it is also generally used.

ENCAMPMENTS.   An old soldier, and an experienced traveller, will always choose
Camp Rules.
the encamping ground himself; as not only his comfort, but very often his safety, will depend upon his selection.

If he is in a hostile country, "*where might is right,*" and he considers his party strong enough to hold their own, in case of an attack from predatory tribes, he will pitch his camp upon an eminence, sufficiently near to water to command its easy approach, and far enough from any cover that might conceal an enemy.

He will take care that his tents are placed so that the excavations form rifle-pits, arranged to defend each other by cross-fires in case of a sudden rush of the enemy from any quarter. This is a most necessary precaution, and if a strict watch is kept day and night, a camp so constructed, and defended by a few resolute men, armed with breech-loading rifles and revolvers, is a formidable place to assault even with greatly superior numbers.

Should the party be too small to offer much resistance, and its object be to pass through a hostile country without attracting observation, the greatest care must be observed, and if a tent is ever pitched, a hollow in a plain, or a patch of dense wood, must be selected for the camp.

Dry wood, which makes very little smoke, should be burnt, and the horses should always be saddled and ready for a move.

The Camp Guard. Watchers and sentries should be posted on elevations in the daytime, and on low ground at night. They should patrol a short distance from the camp, and, if they hear the slightest noise, ought to lie down with the ear close to the ground, by which means they may often detect an approaching footstep at a considerable distance. Sentries ought to be relieved every two hours, if possible; and even if the number of the party is small, and the duty comes round very quickly, still a strict watch should be always kept. Two men, if properly posted, can command a large extent of ground; and it is better to have two watchers who keep wide awake and on the *qui vive*, than a chain of sleepy sentries. When a man knows that the safety of his skin depends upon his keeping his eyes open, he is generally pretty well on the alert.

CHAPTER VIII.

HINTS TO TRAVELLERS.

MUCH of a traveller's comfort depends upon himself, and the best way of getting on is, *by never anticipating difficulties, and making the best of them when they come.* Many of the inconveniences and privations of " camp life " may be avoided or, at any rate, mitigated by forethought and timely precaution, which is only inculcated by experience; but the charms of a

wanderer's life are so many and varied, that they
amply compensate for any little discomforts that
he may meet with *en route.*

We English are a nation of travellers; and, as
Sam Rogers says, " None want an excuse. If
rich, they go to enjoy; if poor, to retrench; if
sick, to recover; if studious, to learn; if learned,
to relax from their studies. But whatever they
may say, whatever they may believe, they go for
the most part on the same errand; nor will those
who reflect, think that errand an idle one.

"In travelling we improve imperceptibly, not in
the head only, but in the heart. Our prejudices
leave us; seas and mountains are no longer our
boundaries; we learn to love, to esteem, and
admire beyond them. Our benevolence extends
itself with our knowledge, and must we not return
better than we went. The more highly we become acquainted with the institutions of other
countries, the more must we value our own. Yet
the enjoyment of travelling, like other pleasures,
must be purchased at some little expense; and he

whose good humour can be ruffled by every petty inconvenience he may chance to encounter had unquestionably better remain at home."

The traveller should adapt himself to the customs and ideas of the people in whose country he sojourns. He should always be a gentleman in his actions, never in his pretensions, and his real worth will become apparent, even amongst savages. Mental superiority will always command respect, and in the desert a man will not be appreciated the more because his ancestor happened to be a great man, or that he is descended from a king's mistress. They judge him by his actions and his line of conduct.

In travelling through a land where " might is right," although it is as well always to be prepared against treachery, suspicion ought never to be shown by any outward sign.

It is always well to treat the inhabitants of the country through which you travel with familiar courtesy, and much information may be gained by mixing with them and entering into their amusements. It is also advisable to fall into the peculiar customs of the country, as they are generally the best adapted to it, and although sometimes they may be a little inconvenient, it is generally much more so to run counter to them.

A good knowledge of the language is an immense help. The Emperor Charles V. used to say that in proportion to the number of languages a man knew, he was so many more times a man. " A knowledge of the language of the country you travel in is as good as a filled purse; as two pair of eyes, and one pair of ears; for without it the one pair he possesses is likely to be of little use." Addison says, " When a traveller returneth home, let his travel appear rather in his discourse than his apparel or gesture; and in his discourse let him be rather advised in his answers than forward to tell stories; and let it appear that he doth not change his country manners for those of foreign parts, but only prick in some flowers of that he hath learned abroad into the customs of his own country."

Early Rising. He who sleeps with a forest tree for his canopy, a stone for his pillow, and the ground for his bed, is not likely to play the sluggard; and the sportsman who means work will be afoot as soon as the soft blue light of the morning becomes perceptible along the eastern horizon; for he knows that his best chance of falling in with large game is before the sun gets up.

"The Stirrup Cup." The traveller should never start early in the morning upon an empty stomach. On the march, before leaving the bivouac, he should always take a cup of coffee, tea, or "*something*," with a biscuit or crust of bread, to fortify the inner man, as the malarious vapours that rise from the ground have an injurious effect on an empty stomach.

When milk and eggs are procurable, " *Tiger's milk*" is not a bad concoction for resuscitating nature. Recipe—Beat up the yokes of six eggs well, with " *a modicum*," or half-pint of spirit (rum or brandy), three lumps of sugar, a bit of lemon peel cut thin, and a little spice, such as cloves or cardamums. Add a quart of new milk, mix well, grating in the third of a nutmeg, and you will have a stirrup cup for three persons.

In hot weather, "*claret cup*" is not a bad substitute. The following is the recipe of Arab Mac (a celebrated old Indian general, of great racing and sporting notoriety), who gloried in having the finest stud and the best kitchen in India:— " To a bottle of claret add three wine-glasses of cognac, a couple of large table-spoons of sugar, the rind of a lime cut thin, a dozen cloves, the seeds of three cardamum-pods, a quarter of a nutmeg, one green chili, a small sprig of borage, a dozen leaves of mint, and a threatening of lime-juice, or, what is perhaps better, a lime cut into thin slices. Let it stand for twenty minutes, and then add three bottles of cooled soda-water, stirring it up well, and serving it out with a ladle whilst in a state of effervescence." This brew makes a good drink for three people.

Beef tea is also very good for a traveller to

take in the early morning; and when ladies are of the party, it always ought to be ready, as they can often swallow that when they can take nothing solid.

Beef tea is made with lean fresh meat, cut into small pieces the size of dice, put into a " digester" or covered jar, which is again placed in a sauce-pan of water, and allowed to simmer until all the goodness is boiled out of the meat, when the juice extracted should be strained and flavoured with salt and pepper. When fresh meat is not ob-tainable, Liebig's Extract of Meat may be used. This extract contains the nutritious constituents of animal food, one ounce containing the soluble matter of about two pounds of fresh meat. Very good beef tea is made by dissolving a dessert-spoonful of the extract in a pint of boiling water, to which salt and pepper should be added.

Striking Camps.

When on the march, unless the head servant can thoroughly be depended upon, it is advisable for one of the party to remain behind, to see the tents struck, the baggage packed, and the mules loaded.

He should also see that no imposition has been attempted by any of the servants, and that there are no complaints " that supplies furnished have not been paid for."

Malarious Districts.   It is highly advisable not to cross low swampy ground, or malarious districts, until at least two hours after sunrise, as by that time much of the noxious vapour so deleterious to health, that rises from the ground during the night and early morning, has been dispelled.   I would, at any time, rather risk the chance of a *coup-de-soleil* by travelling during the day, than expose myself to malaria during the night.

Water.   One of the great causes of sickness in tropical climates is bad water, and the traveller ought to make a rule, *not to drink any that has not been previously boiled and filtered*, if he can possibly avoid it.

In malarious districts, the water, being exposed

to an impure and fœtid atmosphere, absorbs the noxious gases, and becomes impregnated with poison.

Again, in hot climates, water becomes tainted and unwholesome, by filtering through a porous soil full of organic impurities, caused by decomposed animal and vegetable matter; and very often the poisonous ingredients absorbed cannot be detected by the senses, as neither the eye nor the palate of a tired and thirsty traveller are likely to discover the dangerous impregnation.

Water taken from springs and streams is generally better than that of pools, as still water soon becomes putrid, and full of a variety of living animals and vegetables.

The best means of rendering such kinds of water wholesome, is by *boiling* and *filtration :* the former process destroys the animalculæ, and the latter clears it from impurities.

Were proper precautions taken by Government, cholera, typhus-fever and dysentery, the scourges of camp-life, would be comparatively unknown :

whereas, under the present *régime*, when our army takes "the field," ten soldiers die of these diseases to one killed in action ; and this state of things is likely to continue, until "the Press" takes up the matter, and forces our inert officials to look a little better after the welfare of our gallant defenders.

To Find Water.　　Travellers are sometimes put to great straits for want of water, whilst exploring the arid wastes of Africa, and other thinly inhabited flat countries, where rain seldom falls, and every explorer should accustom himself to read *the signs* that indicate the presence of water.

In a flat country, water may generally be found by digging wells in the beds of rivers, taking care to select the spot just below the junction of a tributary, and also paying attention to the formation and appearance of the sand, as it often indicates the line along which the stream last flowed by a winding undulation.

In the bends of a river, deep holes are often formed by the force of the current, where water sometimes remains in pools long after the stream has ceased to run; and such places may often be discovered by following up the fresh tracks of animals. Should these be dry, wells must be sunk in the places where the ground appears to be the lowest.

In mountainous districts small springs are generally found amongst primary rocks; but after a long drought, search should be made in the water-courses that wind through the bottom of the deepest ravines, where pools of water often remain all the year round. Should these prove dry, there is no alternative but to dig in the places where water appears to have been last; and the most likely places are often indicated by the greenest vegetation, or by plants that in that country are usually found near water.

Well-sinking. In sinking wells, the presence of water is indicated by moist sand or earth, before it makes its appearance, as—unless a spring is struck by chance—the water takes some time to filter through the sides of the well, and at first it generally collects very slowly.

In sinking wells in the beds of rivers in Africa, I have had to construct basket-work gabions to prevent the sand from falling in as fast as I dug it out, and sometimes I have had to work very cautiously on account of falling in with " quick-sands."

Signs of
Water.
In searching for water, a line should be formed, and the most insignificant sign must not be overlooked. The fresh track of animals may be followed when they appear to converge, more especially if different species have passed over the ground in the same direction. Flights of birds should be watched, as the feathered race generally drink morning and evening; whenever they are numerous, water cannot be far off.

All animals in a wild state make for water by instinct, but when domesticated they generally appear to lose the faculty; although, sometimes, I have seen horses, oxen, and dogs start off in a bee-line to a pool of water in a country where they had never been before.

In following up the trail of a wounded animal, I have often come unexpectedly across a stream, or pool; as the loss of blood causes intense thirst, and, if not disabled or too closely followed up, most animals will seek for water, and even drink until they fall dead. I have seen both antelope and elephant do this.

In some of the most arid parts of Africa, there are certain plants full of sap, which antelope are very fond of, and sometimes, in case of emergency, I have kept my mouth moistened, and my lips from sticking together, by chewing the pulp. At other times, when very hardly pressed, I have drank the liquid contained in the paunch of different animals I have killed.

" Habit is second nature," and the more a man drinks, the more he wants: a hunter should accustom himself to drink at his morning and evening meals only ; and he ought to be able to go through a hard day's work, even under a tropical sun, by only moistening his mouth from time to time with a couple of spoonfuls of boiled water, or, what is better still for quenching thirst, cold weak tea, without milk or sugar.

Horses and cattle should be accustomed to drink out of a trough, if possible, otherwise when the only water obtainable has to be drawn from shallow wells in the beds of rivers, they will fill them up and cause much extra labour. When travelling with waggons or baggage animals, a small force-pump and hose, as previously described, ought always to be carried,

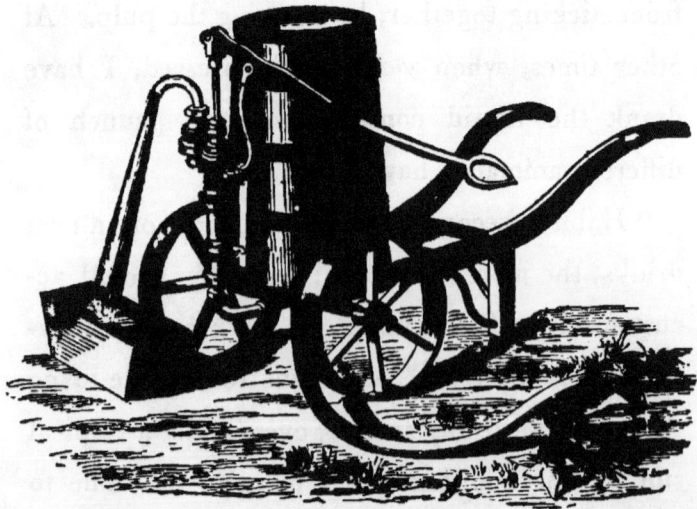

Pump, Hose, and Trough.

as with it the animals are watered with far less labour, and the water in the wells remains undisturbed.

Hard and Soft Water. Soft water is preferable to hard water for all culinary purposes. Monsieur Soyer, the celebrated artist in cooking, declared that where, with soft water, five cups of tea might be made, only three cups could be got with hard water, from equal quantities of the leaf. Soft or distilled water, he says, has an extraordinary power in obtaining a full extract. Vegetables cooked in soft water are quickly done, and the flavour of the vegetables is in the water; whilst those cooked in the hard water never become tender, nor does the flavour go into the water. In extracting the juice or gravy from meat, soft water does it quickly and well; but hard water, instead of opening the meat, seems to draw it closer together, and to solidify the albumen, whilst it fails to extract the true flavour of the meat. For bread-making, soft water is of great importance.

The effect of hard water on animals is very apparent. Horses have an instinctive love for soft water, and they refuse hard water if they can possibly get soft. Hard water produces a rough and staring coat on horses, and renders them liable to gripes.

Summer Beverage.   Pure fruit syrups, such as manufactured by Sainsbury, 176, Strand, when mixed with cold water, or soda water, when you have it, form a very delicious and refreshing beverage in hot weather.

The best way of cooling the water, when ice is not to be procured, is to wrap the bottle or vessel containing it in a wet cloth, and expose it to a current of air, allowing the rays of the sun to shine on it, when practicable. *The cloth must be kept wet, and thoroughly cover the vessel.*

The principle fruit syrups which will keep in tropical climates are lemon, orange, raspberry, strawberry, apple, and red and black currant.

Servants and Followers.   Much of a traveller's comfort depends upon the capabilities of his servants, and my experience leads me to believe that it is much better to gain their confidence by kind treatment, and showing that you have an interest in their welfare, than by harsh measures and "badgering." If you look after their comfort they will look after yours, and a kind and considerate master makes a devoted follower. Always listen to your followers' complaints, whether real or imaginary: if they are real, remedy them; if imaginary, reason with them patiently, and point out the fallacy of their arguments. Make yourself thoroughly acquainted with their character and manners, then it is not difficult to remove their prejudices.

Should insubordination show itself amongst your people, *investigate the cause thoroughly before you act, then be very firm;* in such cases half-measures will not do.

Should punishment be absolutely required, let it be severe and summary, as the example will be greater, and it will be more seldom required. Never strike or flog a man yourself, if you can help it, but let him be punished by one of his fellows, in your presence. It has a better effect.

Reward your followers liberally for extra services. Tobacco, grog in moderation, should be served out in the evening, when they behave properly.

Do what you can to keep them cheerful, by promoting merriment amongst them. I like to hear my fellows sing and chaff good-humouredly amongst themselves as they work; and I believe in an old Indian saying, "A light heart can carry an elephant; a long face stumbles under the weight of his turban."

In India and Africa I never make any objection to my followers being accompanied by their women, as I rarely found them cause any delay whilst on the march, and they were often very useful. Besides, they keep the camp lively and the men contented; and even if they occasion " a row" now and again, it does not much matter, for it serves to break the monotony.

The Watch-fire.

When upon a hunting excursion, and very often whilst campaigning, it has been an established custom for my people to assemble round the watchfire in front of my tent at sunset, and, if possible, I always attend myself, and see that my head-servant goes round and distributes to each man his rations for the next day, an allowance of tobacco, and, if I have it, a glass of grog.

After the distribution I always make a point of asking if all my people are satisfied and if anyone has a grievance or complaint to make, I endeavour to settle it then and there.

Then those who have charge of my animals, such as horses, mules, bullocks, sheep, goats, dogs, and poultry, inform me as to their condition; whilst my head-servant arranges matters concerning the commissariat—an important arrangement when there are many mouths to fill, and rather a responsible one when all the party depend upon their master's gun for food.

The orders for the morrow are then given, the line of route settled, and each man is made to understand what he has to do.

Business settled, the events of the day and the prospects of the morrow are talked over; the habits of wild animals and hunting exploits are discussed; tales are told, songs chanted, and anyone of the party may join in the conversation.

During my wanderings in differents parts of the world my followers have presented a great diversity of appearance, and I have had to do with all kinds of characters; but I found the same line of conduct answer for all, no matter what nation, tribe, or caste they belonged to, and the result of my experience is contained in the following advice: Treat them kindly, pay them fairly, listen to them patiently, humour their prejudices, respect their feelings, do not interfere with their religion; and after a short time you will find that you have gained their confidence, and in your hour of need they will not desert you. When master and servants understand each other, and pull together, "camp life" is the happiest existence I know of.

My "gatherings" have often been a motley crew—a rough and reckless lot of desperate men, of different colours, race, and creed, bound by no tie, and heeding no law—yet perfect unanimity always existed amongst them, and many a jovial night have we passed reclining round the watch-fire after a hard day's work, a sharp skirmish, or a great hunt, when wild songs were sung, strange tales were told, and many a hoarse peal of merriment rang through the night-air, as the jest went round. Loudly we laughed, and little we recked for the morrow.

Hints in Case of Illness. The two great maladies that a sportsman is liable to in malarious regions are fever and dysentery, both of which, if not checked, are apt to end fatally.

Fever. Fever in its mildest form is generally intermittent—that is, there are intervals of health between the attacks; but as

P 2

the disease becomes more aggravated, it assumes the remittent form, and the symptoms only remit, change their aspect, and do not disappear.

Symptoms.   Fever rarely lays its victim prostrate at once. The malarious poison that engenders it has a period of incubation, and breaks out some days after the primary symptoms are evinced—which are, a sense of lassitude and languor, accompanied by yawning and stretching, restlessness, want of sleep, loss of appetite, dull eyes, dizziness, and an incapacity to concentrate the ideas; chills come over the body, and a dull heavy pain racks the loins and kidneys, which often cease to act. Then comes intense headache, cramps which seem to draw up the body, and the hot stage, which often brings on delirium and a state of coma; from which condition the patient either awakes in the next world, or finds himself bathed in profuse perspiration, greatly prostrated, but relieved from pain.

Treatment.

Then is the time to take quinine in as large doses as the system will bear. Should no medical advice be at hand, and the patient be alone in the bush, he cannot do wrong, when in that stage, by taking quinine until his head feels so dizzy that everything appears to turn round, keeping himself covered up, and only drinking hot weak lemonade, so as make him perspire as much as possible.

Sometimes the fever is killed at once by this sharp but severe treatment; but at others, attack comes after attack, and paroxysm follows paroxysm, each one leaving the patient weaker than the last, until the crisis is passed and the disease wears itself out, and gradually becomes weaker in its shocks, or, on the other hand, its victim sinks under it, and passes away in a state of insensibility.

Precautions.

In tropical climates, delays are dangerous, and the slightest symptom should be immediately met with decided and energetic treatment. Constant doses of quinine should be taken daily, more especially when exposed to the dew, rain, night-air, or the malaria engendered by winds blowing over swampy ground or decomposed vegetation.

Dysentery.

My experience leads me to believe that the only cure for dysentery is immediate removal out of tropical climates ; otherwise, it almost always ends fatally.

Treatment.

Upon the first symptoms, take an emetic of ipecacuanha, and in the morning a mild aperient (as 15 grains of rhubarb and 2 grains of calomel) ; on the following day 2 grains of ipecacuanha, with a quarter of a grain of opium, three or four times within the twenty-four hours, eating nothing but plain boiled rice sweetened with sugar.

If this does not stop the complaint, and the tenesmus gives the well-known sign of decided dysentery, a dose of 20 grains of calomel with a quarter-grain of opium should be taken, which must be followed next morning with a dose of castor oil. This generally cuts the matter short ; but it

is as well to follow it up with 2 grains of ipecacuanha, and ½-grain of opium, four times within the
twenty-four hours, for two or three days after:
chlorodyne is also of great service.

Ophthalmia. This disease is often brought on
by sudden transition from excessive
dryness to damp; glare from the snow or desert;
or from dust and sand being blown into the eyes.
In cases of inflammation of the eyes, first remove
the irritation with warm-water fomentations; then
bathe with a lotion composed of 2 grains of sulphate of copper dissolved in an ounce of distilled
or rose water; and for the first stage of ophthalmia, drop into the eye one or two drops of the
following lotion: 10 grains of sulphate of zinc in
one ounce of distilled or rose water.

Of course I need not observe, that in case of
any disease of the eye making its appearance,
the first thing to be done is to obtain the best
medical advice.

My hints are only intended for adoption when
no surgeon is at hand.

USEFUL RECIPES.

To render Shooting Boots Waterproof.

Mix a pint of drying oil, two ounces of yellow wax, two ounces of turpentine, and half an ounce of Burgundy pitch, carefully over a slow fire. Lay the mixture whilst hot on the boots with a sponge or soft brush, and when they are dry lay it on again and again, until the leather becomes quite saturated—that is to say, will hold no more; let them then be put away, and not be worn until they are perfectly dry and elastic; they will afterwards be found not only impenetrable to wet, but soft and pliable, and of much longer duration. Or, take of equal quantities of beeswax and mutton suet, and melt them together in an earthen pipkin over a slow fire; lay the mixture while hot on the boots, which ought to be made warm also; let them stand before the fire a short time, for them to soak the preparation in, and then put them away until quite cold; when they are so, rub them dry with a piece of flannel, in order not to grease your blacking-brushes. If you black them well before you put the mixture on, you will find them take the blacking much better afterwards.

To Preserve Meat.

The natives of India preserve meat, which they call " Ding-ding," by cutting it into long strips, into which they rub salt, ground spices, and then dry in the sun until it becomes as dry as a board.

When required for use, it is allowed to soak in water for a couple of hours to soften, and is then broiled over embers, when it is not at all unpalatable, and often constituted the principal part of a Shekarry's fare whilst on trail.

The Rasp Tip Trap.

The Rasp Tip Trap, invented by Mr. Pringle, of Alnwick, is one of the best for catching small animals alive. The animals are caught between two convex surfaces, as between the fore and middle fingers of the hand when half-closed, and so securely held that escape is almost impossible. No bones are fractured, nor muscles lacerated by the action of the trap.

To Destroy Flies.   Put a handful of quassia into a white basin, and pour a pint of boiling-water over it; let it cool, and sprinkle a little sugar over it as a greater inducement. It will draw away and kill all flies.

CHAPTER IX.

"HINTS TO SPORTSMEN."

Deer-Stalking—Chamois and Ibex Hunting—Feline Animals—
Elephant-Hunting—Pig-Sticking—Dumb Companions.

Deer-
Stalking. THERE is no animal more shy or
solitary by nature than the stag. He
takes alarm from every living thing in the forest;
the slightest sound, be it only the fall of a leaf or
the scratching of a jungle fowl, will scare and set
him off in a moment. Except in certain embar-
rassed situations, *they always run up wind*, their
great security lying in their extreme keenness of
scent, for they can smell a taint in the air at an
almost incredible distance.

When a hart is disabled and run down by dogs,
and he feels that he cannot escape by speed, he

will choose the best position he can, and defend himself to the last extremity with his antlers. Powerful dogs may pull down a full-grown stag when running and breathless, but not a *cold hart* (one that has not been wounded) when he stands at bay, for he takes such a sweep with his antlers that he could exterminate a whole pack, should they attack in front only.

Deer, like many other animals, seem to foresee every change of weather, for they leave the hills and descend into the plains whenever any rough weather is about to take place.

The deer-stalker should not only be able to run like an antelope, but he should possess the bottom of an Arab horse, to enable him to keep the game in view; he should be able to creep like a leopard, and to run with his back bent almost double, and at a pinch to wriggle himself along the ground, *ventre à terre*, like an eel. He should be able to wade or swim torrents, to keep his footing on slippery water-worn stones, remembering, if he does fall, to keep his rifle dry, whatever becomes of himself. He should never go *rashly* to work, keeping always *cool, wary,* and *steady,* never allowing any untoward circumstances to interfere with his equanimity and self-possession.

Before commencing operations, he should carefully survey his line of route, marking any cover that inequalities in the ground, or bushes, rocks, etc., might give. I need not add, that temperance and moderation go a long way to keep *the hand in* and the nerves steady. When I first began deer-stalking, my mentor endeavoured to instil the following general rules in my mind, and several years' subsequent experience has proved to me that his theory is correct. *Be on your ground betimes in the morning; consult the clouds, and keep well to the leeward, even if you have to make a circuit of miles; be silent as the grave; when you step on stones or dry leaves, etc., tread as lightly as a ghost; keep under cover; exercise extreme judgment in approaching your game, which is a happy mixture of wary caution combined with prompt decision and boldness of execution. . Memo.—All this is useless, if you do not use straight powder.*

Hunting the chamois, ibex, and Chamois and Ibex Hunting. creatures of that class, although intensely exciting sport, is the most difficult of all deer-stalking, and proves the severest test of the qualifications of a hunter ; for not only are these animals exceedingly shy and watchful, but they are also gifted with remarkably keen sight, and their senses of smelling and hearing are developed to an extraordinary degree. From the almost inaccessible nature of the ground on which they are found, he who would take their spoils should be endued with great strength, perseverance, and endurance, besides which he must have the agility of a mountaineer and a steady head, or he can never follow up his game to their haunts, along narrow ledges of scarped rocks and beetling heights, where a false step or a moment's giddiness would entail certain destruction. There can be no doubt but that intense excitement takes away all dread of danger, for I have seen it exemplified many times, not only on the hunting-ground but also on the field of battle. An ardent hunter, like a daring soldier, possesses a mental energy superior to all thought of peril; for, seeking only the attainment of his purpose, he pursues his course with that dogged stubbornness, inflexibility of purpose, and recklessness of self-preservation that make him invincible, and ensure success in the end.

Chamois, ibex, mouflon, burrul, gooral, surrow, thaar, markore, oves-ammon, and other gregarious animals of the wild goat or sheep species, are generally found amongst the rugged crags of the loftiest ranges, their food chiefly consisting of the different mosses and short crisp delicate herbage indigenous to high altitudes.

They seem little affected by cold, for in the daytime they remain in the most secluded and inaccessible spots, far above the limits of vegetation, and in the evening move downwards towards their feeding grounds. In summer the males separate from the females, and in a body resort to the higher regions. Generally speaking the females are very inferior in size to the males, and have much smaller horns.

A wary old buck, who has often quite a patriarchal appearance, is generally chosen as the leader of the herd; and if he sees anything suspicious, or catches a taint in the air, a peculiar whistle alarms the rest, causing them to collect together and remain on the alert, and on a repetition of the signal away they scamper, always ascending or descending a slope in an oblique direction. Sometimes I have seen an old female lead the herd, and on such occasions I have always found it extremely difficult to get within range, as they are doubly cunning.

Feline Animals.   Lions, tigers, panthers, leopards, and animals of this genus, are generally hunted either by stalking, beating, sitting up by water, or near the carcass of some animal they have killed.

The great secret necessary to ensure success in this kind of shooting is never to pull trigger unless certain of striking the game in a vital spot, and again, always to keep a shot in reserve, in case of a wounded animal charging.

I need not say that extreme coolness is as much required as accuracy of marksmanship, and anyone who feels " that he even has nerves " had better confine his attentions to game that will not retaliate when wounded.

None of the feline race, with the exception of man-eaters, which are few and far between, will attack men, unless provoked. They always avoid his presence, and the taint even of his footstep in the forest will often make them turn aside and leave the neighbourhood.

These animals are all very tenacious of life, and the hunter should always endeavour to shoot them either through the brain or the heart. I have often dropped them stone-dead with a bullet right between the eyes, or by aiming just behind the shoulder-blade, as the fore-arm moves forward in walking.

Elephant-Hunting.   Any sportsman who is a fair shot, cool, steady, persevering, and active, may count upon killing heavy bags of most kinds of game with tolerable certainty; but he who would slay the elephant in his trackless jungle-home must have other qualities combined, or he will fail in his attempt.

The elephant-hunter must have a thorough knowledge of the nature and habits of that sagacious animal, whose keenly-developed senses far exceed that of any other denizen of the forest; he must be well acquainted with its peculiar structure and anatomy, or his bullet, however true, will never reach the vital part with any certainty; he must be an adept at "tracking," or following spoor, and in the understanding of *jungle signs*, which, although a natural gift to the red men of the Far West and Indian jungle-tribes, is only acquired by intense study and long practice; he must be patient and enduring,

satisfied with hard fare and short commons, as he
will often have to subsist wholly upon his gun,
with the ground for his bed, and a forest tree for
his canopy. He should feel with the great poet,
that "there is society where none intrudes;"
for he must often be content with nature and his
own thoughts as companions, and he must not let
his spirits be depressed by the solitude and
intense stillness of the deep jungle.

The hunter must sleep like a hare, always on
the alert, ever prepared and watchful; for he
never knows what he may meet, or the danger a
moment may bring forth. Inured to peril, he
must never be cast-down or faint of heart; or he
had better not attempt to follow up the spoor of
the elephant to his haunts in the dense, deep
jungle, where the rays of the sun seldom
penetrate, and the woodman's axe was never
heard—where the deadliest of fevers lurk in
places the most beautiful to the eye; and where,
with the exception of certain times in the year,
the air and the water are poisoned by malaria,

and impregnated by the exhalations of decayed
leaves and decomposed vegetable matter, en-
tailing certain death to the hunter, were he
tempted to follow up his perilous calling out of
season.

Hog-hunting, or pig-sticking, as

Hog-Hunting.

carried out in India, is a truly regal
sport, being the incarnation of all that is exciting.
It combines all the attractions of fox-hunting
with the excitement of steeple-chasing, height-
ened by that intense fascination which the presence of danger only can inspire.   It is considerably over twenty years since I took my
maiden spear, yet there are times when every
incident of that memorable day comes vividly
before me, and in my mind's eye I see the well-
remembered forms of my old associates in the
forest and the field, and think I hear their joyous
voices resounding in my ears.   In both the
Deccan and the Nugger Hunts, after Her Majesty's health had been drunk, Bob Morris's chant
was ever " the opening lay," so I give the words.

THE BOAR.

The boar, the mighty boar's my theme,
  Whate'er the wise may say—
My morning thought, my midnight dream,
  My hope throughout the day;
Youth's daring spirit, manhood's fire,
  Firm hand and eagle eye,
Must they acquire who dare aspire
  To see the wild boar die!

Chorus.

  Then pledge the boar, the mighty boar,
    Fill high the cup for me,
  Here's luck to all who fear no fall,
    And the next gray boar we see.

We envy not the rich their wealth,
  Nor kings their crowned career;
The saddle is our throne of health,
  Our sceptre is the spear.
We rival, too, the warrior's pride,
  Deep stained with crimson gore;
For our field of fame's the jungle side,
  And our foe the jungle boar.
    Chorus—Then pledge the boar, &c.

When age hath weakened manhood's powers,
  And every nerve unbraced,
These scenes of joy will still be ours,
  On memory's tablet traced;
And with the friends whom death hath spared,
  When youth's wild course is run,
We'll tell of the dangers we have shared,
  And the tushes that we have won.
    Chorus—Then pledge the boar, &c.

Dumb Companions. If I have endeavoured to impress upon the mind of the traveller the absolute necessity of treating his followers of the human species with consideration, if he has any regard for his own personal comfort, how much more strongly would I urge him to look after the welfare of those servants who cannot complain when they are neglected or ill-treated, or leave his service if they are dissatisfied with it. I refer to his horses and dogs.

Animals appreciate kindness as well, if not better than men; and patience and gentle treatment will do much more in the breaking in of a horse or a dog, than harsh measures and beating.

During the wild life I have been leading for many years, my faithful companions of the brute creation have borne a conspicuous part; and it has ever been my maxim to endeavour to make them look upon man as their friend, and I teach them to obey me from love rather than fear. Vice is engendered by ill-treatment—kindness is never thrown away.

"Feed your horse well, groom him properly, work him with moderation, and he will do you good service," was General Sir Walter Raleigh Gilbert's advice to every youngster on joining his regiment; which precept the veteran carried out in practice, and the consequence was, that in the pursuit of the Seikh army, his nags were in the best condition of any in the force.

I am of opinion that the manner of living of a dog has as much to do in bringing out his qualities as the mere education or breaking in; for instance, Ponto, a favourite hound who was my companion for several years in the woods, by living constantly with his master instead of in the kennel, sleeping near him either in the bungalow or by the watch-fire, and seeing and hearing everything that went on, had not only learnt the meaning of what he saw, but also, in a most wonderful manner, could understand almost everything that was said, either relating to himself, the ordinary routine of camp life, or his duty in the field. He knew that it was my

custom before I got up in the morning to have
cooled soda-water in cantonment, or black coffee
in camp; and if the servant whose business it was
to prepare it happened to oversleep himself, I
had only to tell Ponto, and he would rouse him
at once, distinguishing him from the rest of the
servants without the slightest hesitation, although
a dozen of them might be lying on mats in the
verandah, all entirely enveloped in the same kind
of white chedder or sheet. He also knew most
of my people by name, and would bring them to
me whenever I ordered him. After all kinds of
game, small as well as large, I never saw his
equal; for whenever anything was afoot, by
watching his master's looks, he seemed to understand his meaning. He would retrieve a
snipe, or track a wounded tiger, with equal
certainty; in the latter case, leading his master
fearlessly and quietly a pace in advance along
the trail with the greatest precision and address.
When out deer-stalking, he would creep along by
my side with the greatest caution, never showing

himself, or making the slightest noise. When I
halted he lay down, and after I had fired, if the
quarry was only wounded, he would follow up
the shots with the most untiring perseverance,
singling out the wounded animal from the rest
of the herd, and never leaving the trail, whatever obstacles he might encounter *en route*, until
he brought him to bay, when, showing the
greatest address in avoiding the horns, he would
pin him by the throat and strangle him; or
when the deer was too powerful for him alone—
which was rarely the case, except when only
slightly wounded—he would show great cunning
and generalship in attracting its attention, so as
to prevent its escape, giving tongue until I came
up. When he had killed the game, or if he
found it dead, he would trot back, look up in my
face with a peculiar expression, whine with delight, and then lead me up to the spot where he
had left it. His great delight was large game
hunting; and, although he always preferred
accompanying me on such occasions, yet he would

go with anyone else if I ordered him, looking to
him only for orders whilst with him. I think he
sometimes looked upon snipe-shooting in the hot
weather as rather a bore; for—although he never
seemed to get fatigued in the forest—after some
hours' tramping through the paddy fields and
mud, I have seen him quite done up, and heard
him growl and grumble as he went along, as if
he thought *le jeu ne vaut pas la chandelle.* He
looked upon an indifferent shot with the most
supreme contempt, and the manner in which he
showed his indignation at bad shooting was sometimes highly amusing. In cantonment he lived
on terms of friendship with numerous kinds of
tame animals, against which in their wild state he
was accustomed to wage war ; and young bears,
hunting leopards, deer, antelope, monkeys, mon-
geese, pea-fowl, and partridge, that I kept about
the house, were allowed to wander unmolested,
although he seemed to wish to keep aloof from
them, and never encouraged any undue famili-
arity. With Gooty, my favourite Mahratta pony,

however, the case was very different, for the
reciprocal affection between these two faithful
servants was something extraordinary.

Ponto used to visit the pony in his stall many
times during the day, often carrying to him
biscuits or scraps of bread from his own food,
and Gooty would neigh and whinny in recog-
nition of the dog's whine. With the rest of my
canine followers he was ever the acknowledged
leader, although he used to assume quite an
aristocratic bearing with them, seeming at all
times to prefer his master's society to their diver-
sions. Even my huge Poligar hounds, who were
almost as big as donkeys, used to pay him the
most deferential respect; and I have often been
much struck with the extraordinary power he
had in communicating to them his ideas and
wishes.

I may very fairly attribute much of the success
I have had in large game shooting to the un-
erring instinct of my dogs in tracking. My dogs
never left my heel in the forest, except when set

on trail. On scent, no jungle, however thick, or rocks, however steep, could check their course; no stream, however rapid, could discourage them; they would enter without splashing, cross and double about from bank to bank, until they recovered the scent, and when they came up with their quarry, would keep him at bay until I had time to get up. With a good horse, a good dog, and a good gun, there are lands where a man who knows how to use them may live in luxury, without ever feeling the depressing effects of that baneful disease, "impecuniosity."

CHAPTER X.

HINTS TO NATURALISTS.*

Mammalia—On Skinning and Preserving Animals of this Class—
On Preserving the Skeletons—Birds—On Skinning, Preserving, and Packing, so as not to Injure the Plumage—
Birds' Eggs—Nests—Reptiles and Fish, How to Preserve
them—Insects, Where to Find them, How to Catch them,
and the Best Manner of Preserving them—Butterflies
and Moths—Beetles—Spiders, Scorpions, etc.—Crustacea—
Sponges and Corallines—Star-fish and Echini—Land and
Fresh-water Shells—Marine Shells, and Where to Find them
—Dredging—The Collector's Note Book—Instruments required—Recipe for Arsenical Soap, and How to Use it.

Mammalia.
SMALL animals of this class may
either be skinned or inclosed entire
(an incision being previously made in the under
side of the animal) in jars or barrels, which are

---

* The author is indebted to Mr. S. Stevens, the naturalist, for
this valuable compilation of practical information.

to be filled up with some spirituous liquor, as gin, or, what is preferable when it can be procured, proof-spirit diluted with half its bulk of water. If no spirit can be had, strong brine must be adopted. In respect to their retaining their natural colour, brine is even preferable to spirituous liquors for preserving the specimens. To skin the larger mammalia, make an incision in a straight line along the belly, from the vent to the throat, and detach the skin carefully with the knife. The skull and the bones of the legs and feet are to be left; the brain, eyes and tongue must be extracted, and as little fat as possible be suffered to remain adhering to the inside of the skin, which is then to be dressed with arsenical soap, for the mode of making and applying which see note at end. If, however, some fat remain which cannot well be got rid of, strew it over with powdered tan, or the bark of oak, willow, &c., previously to applying the soap. The ears, lips and feet of large mammalia should, when practicable, be well anointed with spirits of turpentine, which will assist their drying and tend to destroy insects : when dry, roll up the skin with the hair innermost, beginning with the head, and put a layer of dried grass or moss between the folds, to prevent its being injured by rubbing. The skin must be occasionally unrolled and examined, and, if practicable, exposed to a hot sun, and fresh spirits of turpentine added. If any symptoms of insects should appear, tobacco (the stronger the better) strewed in the package will be ser•viceable ; and in countries where spices and aromatic drugs can be procured at a reasonable rate, these may be used to great advantage, and even supersede the necessity of applying the arsenical soap. When a very large animal has been killed, under · circumstances which prevent the application of the arsenical soap, the skin should be stretched out on the branches of a tree, to give the air free access to every part of it, and, as soon as it is cold, well dressed on the inside with wood ashes. Entire skeletons (especially of the rarer animals) should be procured when possible. It is not necessary that they should be jointed or set up, but, having removed all the soft parts, boil the bones, and when well dried pack them with moss or grass, or the best packing-stuff at hand, so that they may travel securely. Take especial care that not a bone, tooth, or claw, be lost.

Birds.

With respect to birds, the collector should proportion his shot to their size, so as to injure the skin and feathers as little as possible. As soon as the bird falls, the blood should be carefully wiped up, and cotton placed within the beak to absorb any that might flow from the mouth, and thus prevent its staining the plumage. Birds should be skinned as soon as may be after they are killed, for, if suffered to remain till putrefaction has begun, the feathers fall off. The mode of skinning birds is very similar to that of skinning mammalia, and equal care must be taken both to make the incisions as small as possible and in the least visible parts, and the feathers must be separated so as not be injured by the knife in dividing the skin: the

incision may be made from the vent to the breast:
the head and legs must in all cases be carefully
preserved, and the os coccygis left in the skin,
otherwise the tail-feathers will be liable to drop
out. In packing the skins care must be taken
that the plumage be not injured by contact with
the harder parts, which for that purpose should
be surrounded with cotton, tow, or the best soft
packing material at hand, as dried leaves or grass.
When more than one individual of the same
species can be procured, it is desirable that a
second specimen should be preserved in spirits,
and the same remark applies to the smaller mammalia, and indeed to all the orders. The bird-
skins must be dressed with the same materials as
those of the mammalia, but the arsenical soap—if
used at all—must not be too liberally applied.
As the plumage of birds varies extremely at different periods of their life, and even at different
seasons of the year, it is of great importance to
obtain both sexes, if possible, of all ages, from
the chick just hatched to the adult in its maturest

plumage, and also in their summer and winter liveries. Birds' eggs should also be anxiously sought for, and the species carefully identified: the best method of emptying them is to make a single hole near the middle of the shell, of about an eighth of an inch in diameter, into which a small tube is to be inserted, so as nearly to touch the opposite side of the shell, which, being held with the hole downwards, is easily emptied of its contents, by blowing pretty strongly through the tube: if no more convenient instrument is at hand, a straw will make a very serviceable blow-pipe. Birds' nests should not be neglected; they possess a high degree of interest: the collector should, therefore, take accurate descriptions of the materials, form, and size, of every kind of nest he finds, always being extremely cautious to ascertain the species to which each respectively belongs: he should also make careful drawings of every variety, and even collect such of the smaller nests as possess any peculiarity in point of material, structure, or mode of suspension.

Burnt alum will be found very useful in cleaning the fingers whilst skinning birds and animals, and also applied to those which have a good deal of fatty matter adhering to them.

Reptiles and Fish.
These are best preserved in spirits, each specimen being previously wrapped in a linen cloth; but when too large to be so treated, serpents and fish may be carefully skinned, with the least possible injury to the scales or any of the external organs, and with especial caution not to destroy the form of the skin, which may be preserved by stuffing it tightly with cotton or tow, or by filling it with sawdust, and the skins dried, with the head, feet, and fins on. Instead of being skinned whole, fish may be divided into two nearly equal portions, by an incision passing longitudinally through the vertex of the head, the back and belly, but on one side of the dorsal, caudal, anal, and ventral fins, so as to leave one-half of the animal with the gills and all the organs of motion perfect. Their flesh may then be easily removed

from this portion, and replaced by tow, which will preserve the form of the body. When well dried, this portion is to be carefully packed. On the whole, this method is preferable to all others; and fish thus preserved, when provided with proper artificial eyes, and mounted on flat boards, afford excellent specimens. The upper and lower shells of the tortoise tribe should be separated by dividing the ligamentous or bony portion which unites them on each side, between the fore and hind legs; after which the fleshy parts may easily be removed, the head, legs, and integuments of the body being carefully preserved. As to the lizards and crocodiles, they may be skinned in the usual manner, care being taken not to injure the tails of the former, which are very brittle, or, when not too large, they may be preserved in spirits, which is still better.

The form and colour of the eyes in all the vertebrata, of whatever class, should be carefully observed and noted down the moment they are taken.

Insects. Insects may be found almost everywhere; look especially for all *beetles* under stones, under bark of decayed trees, on the inside of ditto, on felled ditto; on trunks of ditto (especially those that have the sap running from them), by beating the boughs into a net or sheet, smoking under and burning inside hollow trees, on long grass or herbage, on flowers, under rubbish (especially on the slopes of mountains, and in marshy places), under sea-weed at the sea-side, and indeed they are to be found almost everywhere in warm climates, especially in open places in woods, and on the slopes of hills, and are generally most abundant in a light sandy soil, and in and after the rainy seasons: they may be collected either by picking with the hands, or by sweeping and brushing with a net, according to the situation: the larger ones may either be put separately into pill or other boxes, or else immersed at once into a bottle of clear spirit, when they almost immediately die; and may either remain in the spirit, and be sent in this way to England (if possible

changing the spirit just before sending), or else
the same or following day taken out and soaked
for about a quarter of an hour in warm water,
and then laid on blotting-paper a few hours to
dry: after that, either pin and stick in tight in a
well-made box, lined with cork or some soft
wood, or else (if in a dry country) lay carefully
in rows, in a box, on cotton wool: numbers may
be packed this way in layers, between soft paper,
and generally reach England in beautiful condition. The small beetles may also be collected
and sent in the same way, and, if immersed in
spirit, put in a separate bottle from the large
ones; or else when captured put into a phial with
some blotting-paper, and killed on reaching home,
by immersing it in hot or boiling water for a
minute or two, or placing it in the heat of the
sun for a short time: they can then either be
pinned or else packed in soft paper in rows and
layers, as the others, and should not be despised
on account of their small size, as they are frequently more valuable than the larger ones.

Look especially in and near ants' nests in sultry weather, and under bark of trees where ants occur, or under stones, and at the roots of grass, for small beetles.

Butterflies and Moths (Lepidoptera) must be collected with great care, so that the beautiful scales on the wings are not rubbed off or injured, as they then become generally worthless: they may be bred from caterpillars found on various trees and plants (which is an excellent plan, as they are then very perfect), or else caught by the aid of a gauze net: a ring net about 1½ foot in diameter and 2 feet deep, will do very well, attached to a stick 3 to 6 feet long. Woods and wild places are generally the best to find them in; it is necessary to pin them as you take them, which must be done with great care, so that the upper parts of the wings are not rubbed; therefore the collector must be provided with a good large box to stick them in. Some of the large and big-bodied moths will probably not die unless a little oxalic or nitric acid is applied

to them, which may be done by dipping a long
pin or needle into it, and running it down the
body of the insect two or three times, commencing under the mouth; they can then either be
pinned tight in boxes, or else laid between dry
cotton and paper, the same as the beetles; or
when collected, instead of being pinned, put
into three-cornered pieces of paper with the
wings folded up, which is a very good plan when
there is no convenience for carrying boxes. Other
sorts of insects may be caught and killed the
same way, and sent over as before directed, between layers of cotton and paper. No other
insects but beetles should be put into spirits;
and not these when the colours are beautiful,
delicate, and of a chalky texture: the bottle before sending should be *full* of insects, or else
filled up with cotton, so that they cannot shake
about.

Great care must be taken with all insects that
they do not get broken, especially the horns
(antennæ) and legs of beetles, and the antennæ

and wings of the butterflies and moths, for then their value is greatly diminished.

Beetles should always be pinned through the right elytrum, or wing case, so that the pin may come out between the first and second pair of legs; but all other insects may be pierced vertically through the thorax. Great care must also be taken that the boxes containing the insects be left in a dry situation, and the sooner they are transmitted to England the better, previously applying to the inside of the boxes a small quantity of powdered arsenic or camphor, to prevent the attacks of small insects.

Arachnida.—Spiders, Scorpions, and Acari are best preserved in spirits, as well as the Myriapoda, including the Juli, Scolopendræ, and other individuals of the order; but they may be pierced through the thorax (the intestines being carefully removed and replaced by cotton), and pinned tight in boxes, as the insects.

Crustacea.—The marine species may be killed

by being immersed in cold fresh water, and they should be left in it for several hours, to free them from the adhering salt, which, if not well washed out, renders them liable to attract moisture from the atmosphere and injures the specimens. When well washed, separate the upper shells, and remove as much of the fleshy parts as possible; then carefully dry and pack them. The smaller species may be pierced with pins, like insects, if the consequent bulk of the packages be not an objection. Entire Crustacea may be preserved in strong spirits or brine.

Sponges and Corallines.—Search the line of sea-weed at high-water mark, and the more the latter are covered with small corals and other parasites the better. Never wash them in fresh water, but dry them as they are found. Never wash or squeeze sponges; the fuller they are of gelatinous or fleshy matter the better. Use unwashed small Fuci as packing, dried, but not to crispness: the boxes should be divided into two or three compartments. Corals should never be washed or bleached, but sent as they come from the sea.

Star-Fish and Echini.—These may be either dried or bottled in the saline fluid. If large, plunge them for two or three minutes into boiling water before drying; if small, one minute will be enough. Annelides, Actinia, and other fleshy things, may be bottled with a saturated solution of bay salt, with two grains corrosive sublimate to each quart. Always keep up the strength of the saline solution by the addition of salt as needed.

Land and Fresh-water Shells.—Land shells are found in many places, such as under stones, in clefts of rocks, on the sides of hills and mountains, under decayed wood and trees, on the trunks, roots and leaves of trees and bushes, in decayed vegetable matter, dried leaves and moist, on small plants; in fact, almost every situation produces them except open and cultivated places: where dead specimens are found, living ones cannot be far off. When collected, bring them home and put them in a pail, or some other large vessel, and pour a quantity of cold water over them; then cover up the vessel for two or three hours, which will cause the animals to come out a little (it is necessary to cover them up, or else they will crawl away): when they are a little out, draw off the water, and pour a quantity of boiling water on them, so as to cover them well: let them remain a few minutes to cool a little; then take out the animals with a large pin or needle, as you would a periwinkle: when they are all done, take a soft brush and wash off gently all the dirt and filth from them, and place them in another vessel of fresh water until all are clean; then shake out well the water that is in them, and place them out to dry, with their mouths downwards, but not in the sun: when dry, if they are small, pack them away in small boxes, writing on the cover the locality and situation in which found. Should the shells be rather large, then wrap each shell in a paper by itself, and pack them away in a larger box, with their localities, etc., with care; but never put by a box that is not quite full without adding sufficient cotton or other soft substance to fill it, for such tender subjects should not have play during their transit. In rivers, lakes, ponds, and small streams, will be found many species of shells which—although not handsome—are very interesting; none, therefore, should be left behind, as it may be a cause of regret hereafter. Some of the shells which will be found in the above-mentioned places are of the same form as the land shells; others are like our fresh-water mussel or cockle: they are mostly found in the mud, sometimes in deep water: dead ones are sure to be found on the banks of lakes and rivers; and if you cannot procure living ones, show the natives the dead specimens, and offer them money to get a quantity of living ones. The rivers and pieces of water abound with shells: be diligent in seeking them, and your labours will be most amply repaid. Having collected the fresh-water shells, place them in a vessel, and pour a large quantity of boiling water on them; they do not require to be first put into cold water, as the land shells do: as soon as the water is a little cool, pour it off, take out the animals as before mentioned, wash the shells, etc., etc.; but as the bivalve or fresh-water mussel will open wide as soon as the animal is out, it must be tied close before being put out to dry; if not the hinge will break, and make the shell valueless. Some of the fresh-water shells that are like the snails have a mouth-piece, or operculum, which must be taken care of: the mouth-pieces should be kept in separate packages, and packed with the species of shell to which they belong, as they are of great service in determining the species. Some of the land shells have also a mouth-piece, which should be packed in the same manner. When the bivalve shells are tied up and dry, wrap each of them in a piece of soft paper, pack them in small boxes, and remember localities, habitats, etc., etc.

Marine Shells.—The best time to collect shells on the sea-shore is at the new and full moon, for then the tides make greatest ebb: the collector should be on the spot two hours before low water, with an assistant to help in turning over the large stones, should there be any, under which will be found many species of cowries, buccinums, tritons, mitres, cones, and several species of bivalve shells, also many kinds adhering to the stones, which must be taken off with a knife in a careful manner : several species bore into the stone itself, which must be broken with hammers to get out the shells, or, if the stone be soft, cut it carefully with a hatchet, on doing which many more species will be found : care must be taken to avoid breaking the shells : be always provided with a light basket and a small box in it, in which to put the smaller and more delicate specimens. The stones when turned over must be well inspected, as many will be found covered with marine matter, which makes them appear like the stone itself : collect all, and do not despise them on account of their unmeaning appearance, for amongst them may be new genera and other very rare shells. Many stones at the very lowest ebb will have most shells on them, therefore the collector must not mind getting a little wet. Amongst other sorts will be found chitons, which must be taken off in the same manner as the limpet and other adhering univalves: care must be taken, when at home, to separate them from the other shells; put them into a pail of fresh water, and let them remain there from twelve to twenty-four hours, by which time the salt on the fleshy substance that surrounds them will be well soaked out; then cut out the animal, and wash the shells well, inside and out, from all filth, and throw them into another vessel of fresh water, where let them remain till the whole are cleaned; then place them on a narrow strip of board and bind them down tightly, put them in a shady place to dry, and in three or four days they will be fit to pack.

Among the rocks on the sea-shore, in the crevices and on them, will be found many species of patellas, chitons, murices, etc. Make a careful survey of every rock and stone ; they will amply repay the trouble. All sheltered coves or little bays are the best places in which to find shells : examine these places in preference to others, particularly those in more exposed situations. The first thing to observe when in a new locality is to go along the sands at high-water mark, for many good shells are thrown up by the sea, particularly light bivalves ; any time of the tide will do. Never miss going after a gale of wind, for then many valuable deep-water shells will be found which are not seen at other times. In sheltered bays and places just at the very lowest water-mark will be found, in the sand and mud, various species of bivalve shells, just beneath the surface, and generally in great abundance: do not neglect to collect all and every species, and in plenty.

In collecting shells, whether terrestrial or aquatic, the collector must always give the preference

to live shells—that is, such as are still inhabited
by the living animal—but if they cannot be obtained, dead shells are better than none, though,
for the most part, they are worn and faded.   The
more delicate species must be packed in cotton
,or other soft substance, or, in a default of such, a
.fine sawdust.   Shells containing their animals, as
well as the naked mollusca, must be preserved in
spirits or brine.

Dredging.   It is necessary to have a rope for
the dredge from 2½ to 3 inches (60
fathoms long); a fine sieve, a bucket and a
ladle; a boat with a small anchor and cable (not
less than 30 fathoms), to moor her in the situation
where you are going to dredge; a good stout
canoe to convey the dredge away from the boat
as far as the rope will allow.   The dredge to lie
in the bow of the canoe, mouth upwards, handle
inwards : when it is conveyed as far as the rope
will allow, those in the canoe are to heave—that
is, turn the dredge over gently into the water,
and let it be from five to six minutes, until it is

fairly at the bottom; then haul it on board the boat: should any obstruction—such as a rock, etc.,—prevent its being brought home, place the canoe under the rope and pull her along until the place of obstruction is arrived at; then bring up the dredge, either straight or by taking it a little way back, and let those in the boat haul dredge and canoe towards them until clear of the obstacle: the dredge is to be let down again, and hauled in as before. When the dredge is brought alongside the boat, lift it in, and take out all the mud and sand; half fill the sieve with this, and pour a bucket of water gently on it, the party holding the sieve to shake it gently until all the mud and fine sand has passed through: take out all the larger shells as soon as possible, to prevent their breaking the more delicate ones, and put them into your basket, and the smaller ones into boxes. Should there be many small shells in the sieve, which would take much time picking out, it would be best to throw the sand from the sieve into a basket, and take it home, where it can be inspected more minutely, after having dried it in the sun on paper. The nearer the collector gets to a reef of rocks in sheltered places, the better for shells, as they will lie there for protection; but be careful to throw the dredge clear of the rocks, as it will save a deal of trouble.

The dredge can be made 3 feet 6 inches long and 1 foot wide: the outer edge to be turned outwards about the angle of 30°, and beaten down rather fine: the lower part of the bar should not be less than half-an-inch thick, with holes punched in it from one end to the other, an inch and a-half apart, to lash the bag to: the bag can be fashioned according to the dredge, and made of double bread-bags.

General Remarks.   Every specimen, dry or in spirit, should have a number attached to it, corresponding to one in the collector's note-book, in which he must enter his memoranda concerning it; as for instance:

The country where found,   Habits,

The season when,   Habitat,

Local name.

The collector should be furnished with knives, scissors, scalpels, pliers, nets, a large assortment of pins of various sizes, needles, a hammer, small hatchet, packing-cases (large and small, including cork boxes for lepidoptera and other insects, and a great number of pill-boxes in nests), cotton and paper, and also with a folding-net, hoop-net, water-net, forceps, digger, glass phials, etc., for collecting insects; he must also have a good supply of prussic acid and arsenical soap. The composition and mode of making the latter is as follows:

Camphor	. . . .	5 oz.
Arsenic, in powder	. .	2 lbs.
White soap	. . . .	2 lbs.
Salts of tartar, or subcarbonate of potash	. . . .	12 oz.
Lime, in powder	. . .	4 oz.

Melt the soap completely with heat in a small quantity of water, and add the potash and lime; then remove it from the fire and stir in the arsenic; next add the camphor, previously rubbed to powder, with a little spirit of wine, and mix the whole thoroughly: it should now have the consistence of paste. Preserve it in carefully-closed glazed vessels, labelled " POISON."

To use it, mix the quantity required with cold water to the consistence of tolerably clear soup, and apply it with a brush to the inside of the skins.

CHAPTER XI.

THE FOREST AND THE MOUNTAIN.

Pleasing Recollections—The Primeval Forest—The Fascinations of a Hunter's Life—A Forest Ranger's Qualifications—Forest Scenery—Woodland Streams—Forest Creatures—The Forest during the Different Periods of the Day and Night—The Voices of the Woods—The Ever-changing Face of Nature—Instinct of Animals—Variety of Character—The Language of Animals—"Breathings of Nature"—Weird Music—A Hunter's Lullaby—Mountain Scenery—Mountain Life—The Mountaineer—The Highest Altitudes.

THE forest! How many pleasing recollections of heart-stirring events are associated with that name; how many a glorious day's sport does it recall to mind; how many a dear friend does it bring before me with whom I have bearded the tiger in his lair, tracked the mighty elephant to his haunt in its inmost recesses, and there despoiled him of his trophies. Many a hand I then

clasped has become cold, many a voice I loved
to listen to is hushed for ever, but the forest, the
home we rangers all loved so well, is still un-
changed, and my heart yearns to return to those
well-remembered scenes which I shall now attempt
to portray.

The Primeval Those who have never explored a
Forest. primeval forest can have but a very
faint conception of the mysterious effect that
absence of light and intense depth of gloom
have upon the human mind. The unbroken
silence and utter stillness that everywhere pervades its leafy arches, creates a strange feeling of
awe and loneliness that depresses the spirits and
appals the heart of those who are unaccustomed
to wander in its solitudes; and even the stoutest
heart feels overpowered with a strange sensation
he can neither account for nor explain the first
time he enters, for the voice of the man resounds
with a strange and startling echo, and even the
very hound whines with fear, and couches close
to his master's side, afraid of being left alone.

Solitude is too insufficient a term

The Fascina-
tions of a
Hunter's Life.

to convey an idea of the intensely
overpowering sensation of desolation
and loneliness that pervades these regions; yet,
to the hunter, who is accustomed to sojourn in
their deepest recesses, the wilderness is a home
which he would not exchange for any other; and
as he roams through its boundless expanse of
vendure, with no other companions but the silent
trackers and his dogs, and no guide but a
pocket-compass and certain jungle signs not to
be understood by the dwellers in cities, he
imbibes certain feelings that cannot be entered
into save by those who have themselves experienced the charms and fascinations of "forest
life," and enjoyed its pure and heartfelt pleasures. To him it possesses a peculiar spell, not
to be found elsewhere; and, far away from the
haunts of man, he gives no care to the turmoil
and bustle of the busy world, but loves to study
nature in her grandest form, and silent unsullied

beauty, whilst his heart glows with thoughts that bear him untiring company.

There is a peculiarly exhilarating delight, passing all description, in the wild excitement of this life, which dispels all anxiety, and strengthens the mental and physical energies for the ever-changing scene, delights the eye, and gives pleasure to the intellect, whilst, at the same time, the constant excitement arising from the varied incidents of such a state of existence invigorates the mind and stimulates the powers of thought and observation.

A Forest Ranger's Qualifications. The body, sustained in continued exertion by constant exercise, enables the hunter to maintain his course for days together through the pathless woods, with that dogged stubbornness and inflexibility which is necessary to ensure success in the pursuit of the game he seeks. He moves noiselessly along, without a care as to what he may encounter, for he has implicit confidence in the power of his

trusty rifle; and his vigilant eye, piercing the
shadowy depths of the jungle, leaves no hollow
unsearched, for he and his followers are dependent for their subsistence on their exertions in
the chase.

Nothing is so conducive to the keen develop-
ment of the senses as the constant exertion of
the different faculties during a sojourn in the
jungle, quickness of eye (an indispensable quality in a hunter) and unceasing watchfulness are
there attained; habits of observation are engendered, for anything out of the common immediately attracts attention, and the ear is habituated
to catch the slightest sound.

The hunter should have a thorough knowledge
of the habits of the wild animals he seeks, bearing in mind how suspicious they are, and how
quickly their attention is attracted by unusual
noises, strange traces in the jungle, or even the
taint in the air which the presence of man always leaves behind. The ranger of the forest
experiences a thorough feeling of independence

and a freedom from restraint in these wilds, that contrasts most favourably with the *désagréments* of artificial existence ; and few of those who are fitted to enjoy it, ever quit these scenes to return to civilised life without deep feelings of regret that their unalloyed pleasures are at an end ; and in after life, the murmuring of waters, and the sighings of the wind through the trees, will recall to mind moments of intense interest, and they will ever feel at heart that there is no music so sweet as the wild voices of the woods.

Forest Scenery.   All forests are gloomy, but they have, their comparative degrees of shade, and present a great diversity of appearance. The tall feathery bamboo contrasts most delightfully with the stately teak, ebony blackwood, and other gigantic trees of the primeval forest, where the air, being confined, is generally close and suffocating. The surface of the ground is everywhere thickly strewn with decayed leaves or dead branches, and underneath the trees may be seen the green of young seedlings which spring up by thousands during the rains, but for the most part pine and die, being deprived of light and heat.

In some places the forest becomes more open, dense woods alternating with beautiful verdant glades, and their limits are so well defined, that the scene much resembles the ornamental plantations of an English park; indeed, so much does this similitude strike the Anglo-Saxon stranger, the first time it meets his eye, that he looks around the verdant lawns, shrubberies of evergreen, stately avenues, and embowering groves, fully expecting to see some ancestral manorial mansion, or gray embattled pile, to diversify the landscape, so strongly does it remind him of the home he has left—perhaps for ever.

Every turn in the forest reveals some change. In some places fern flowers and grasses creep fantastically tangled on the sides of darkly frowning crags, and lichen-covered precipices raise their heads above the wave-like looking sea of forest, and present a scene with that depth of colouring

and exquisitely rich tints that Salvator Rosa
loved to paint.

Woodland Streams. Clear pellucid streams and rivulets
are often met. with in the densest
forests; and during the dry season, the hunter
cannot do better than follow their course, as all
kinds of game abound in their immediate neighbourhood.

Their banks are often carpeted with mosses
and lichens of endless variety of tints, whilst
patches of gorgeous flowers are seen amongst
the luxuriant herbage, adding their rich colours,
as if to diversify the sombre appearance the
forest usually wears. In some places they run
through open glades; in others they are completely arched over with dense foliage, forming
an impervious shade over head, the trees on both
sides being laced and bound together with an
infinity of wild vines and gigantic creepers, which
hang in festoons, or lie twisted in snake-like coils
upon the ground.

Gushing through the arches of the forest, the

woodland stream dashes along through scenes of ever-varying loveliness and beauty, with a voice of impetuous freedom and gladness : now, with a pleasant murmur, it rattles over a bed of pebbles ; now, lost to the eye, it glides stealthily through a shady hollow; now it sweeps past the base of huge masses of syenite cliff; dashes over boulders of rock, or creeps silently among moss-covered stones; now, divided by dark, boldly jutting rocks, it is scattered into a score of bubbling rills; now, again united in one broad expanse, a rolling mass of foam, it goes tumbling headlong over a rocky precipice into a boiling abyss below, mingling all its waters in a foaming pool. Joined in its course by a thousand springs and tributary streams, at last it becomes a broad and rapid river, gliding smoothly along, hushed in peace, reflecting the passing cloud, and scarcely ruffled by the freshening breeze; then man builds his habitation by its banks, and forest creatures drink of its waters in fear and trembling.

Forest
Creatures.

Each period of the day has its accustomed visitants, every hour has its "certain signs," that can be read and understood by those only to whom jungle voices are familiar, and who, from long habit and experience, have been enabled to observe and mark the systematic order of Nature's handiwork.

Early Morning in the Forest.

In tropical climates the interval between the first glimmering of dawn and daylight, is very short, and on entering the forest at this hour, jungle-cocks (whose plumage gleams like gold as they run by followed by their dusky seraglio) may be heard crowing merrily on every side, whilst great hooded-owls, like drowsy revellers after their night's carouse, sail hooting, leisurely flapping their wings as they return to their haunts in some hollow tree. As the light increases, the notes of the earliest of the feathered songsters are heard, and troops of monkeys are seen making their way to some pool or stream for their morning draught, but who fly skipping from branch to branch, chattering and showing their teeth as soon as they discover our presence. Now and again, the dun sides of deer flash for an instant before us, as they bound across the open vistas of the forest, and disappear in the densest cover.

Birds of gaudy plumage dart amid the branches, gay butterflies hover about, insects of metallic hue glitter on the leaves, and all Nature seems glad in this highly-favoured spot.

Toucans and gigantic horn-bills, with their awkward flight, pass from tree to tree in search of the reptiles and small animals on which they feed; and long lines of flamingoes, with their magnificent rose-coloured plumage, pelicans, herons, storks, and ibis, may be seen in long lines wending their way towards their feeding grounds.

In certain seasons, long before sunrise, elk are heard bellowing, and their loud cries of defiance resounding from every side of the forest, might, by unaccustomed ears, be mistaken for the roaring of much more dangerous animals, so hoarse and hollow do they sound.

All nocturnal animals return to their haunts in

T

the deep jungle on the first appearance of dawn,
when the jungle-cock sounds the " réveille."
Bison and deer retire slowly from the open glades
where they have pastured during the night, and
seek the shade of the thick cover.

At this early hour there is generally a cool
breeze, and the morning air is fresh and bracing;
but very shortly the whole of the eastern horizon
glows with ruddy lustre, and the sun bursts forth
in a blaze of living light, and seems to travel on
his way in the heavens with much more rapidity
than in northern climes. This is the moment for
the lover of the beautiful to see the forest, for
the dewdrops on the leaves and ground sparkle
like brilliants, and at no other time are the varied
colours of the verdure so vivid. The lights and
shades show to the best advantage, and a peculiarly harmonious charm reigns over the whole
face of Nature, which must strike upon the heart
even of the most apathetic spirit, and make him
feel, with the great poet, that.

" There is a pleasure in the pathless woods."

Noon in the Forest.

During the intense heat of the day, whilst the sun is still high above the meridian, all animated nature seems to yield to his overpowering influence. A strange stillness, a profound silence, reigns throughout the forest, which in early morning seemed to teem with life and motion. Every living creature disappears into the deepest shade of the woods, in order to escape from the exhausting heat and oppressive glare; except, perhaps, the eagle, hawk, and falcon, who are seen hovering overhead in circles, like specks in the cloudless sky, or skimming, with strange wild cries, over the tops of the jungle in search of their prey, and the green enamelled dragon-flies that still flit over the water from leaf to leaf. Then the sturdy hunter, overcome with lassitude, suspends his toil, and seeks the grateful shade of some gigantic forest-tree or overhanging rock, where he reposes until the mid-day heat is passed, whilst his dog, also sharing in the universal languor which seems at that hour to oppress the whole face of nature, lies panting upon the ground, with his legs extended to the utmost, and his tongue hanging far out of his mouth.

The weary hours roll on, and Nature revives: the woods again resound with the melody of the voice of birds; butterflies, of varied hue, flutter across the open glades; bees flit from flower to flower; and lustrous beetles, exhibiting metallic hues of green and blue, that rival the deepest shades of the emerald and the sapphire, hover round in circles, making a peculiar booming noise from the flutter of their wings. Myriads of insects keep up a perpetual hum in the solitudes of the jungle, and other gentle sounds murmur softly from every side, like spirits in the air, and produce an effect singularly strange, soothing, and dreamy. At times, above this jungle melody, may be distinguished the distant cry of the peacock, the shrill wild note of jungle-fowl, the call of the coppersmith, the tapping of the woodpecker against some hollow tree, the chattering of a troop of monkeys as they pass in the dis-

tance, bounding from bough to bough ; the peculiarly soft and melancholy note of the turtle-doves,
as they flutter in pairs from tree to tree ; or the
shrill screams of flights of paroquets, whose brilliant plumage shines with exquisite lustre in the
light of the sun, as they dash close past, uncon-
scious of danger in their forest home.

Evening in   As the day declines, birds of all
the Forest.
kinds are seen returning homeward
from their distant feeding-grounds ; pelicans rise
heavily on their unwieldy wings from the
marshes, and wend their way to their nests on
the highest trees in some secluded spot.   Flying-
foxes leave the shady grove where they have hung
suspended during the heat of the day, and are
seen in numbers darkening the sky as they roam
through the twilight ; whilst multitudes of bats
flit about in all directions in search of the insects
on which they feed.

As the sun sets, insects of all kinds issue from
their retreats, and mosquitoes are constantly heard
buzzing about, increasing in the audacity of their

attacks as the night wears on. The shrill voices of innumerable crickets, the croaking of frogs, and the continual hum of other insects, keep up a perpetual serenade long after darkness has covered the earth.

The tuneful songsters ceased their warbling, and the woods no longer resounded with the sharp strokes of the woodpecker; but the nighthawk was on the wing, and darted swiftly to and fro after the moths, which at that hour flit about in great numbers. The air becomes redolent with the fragrance of numberless flowering shrubs, which seem to emit a double perfume towards the close of day. The evening deepens into twilight, the twilight darkens into night, and the stars with their mild radiance seem as if they strove to eclipse the lingering rays of sunset. At length the mighty forest becomes silent, and no sound reaches our ears save the occasional chirping of a cricket, the dismal hooting of the horned howl, the howling of troops of jackals, or the melancholy booming of the great hill-monkey.

As the night wears on, the tall trees can hardly be distinguished one behind another, as they loom darker and darker against an indefinable background.

Hundreds of flying-foxes glide silently through the night air, like evil spirits of darkness ; and the harsh cry of alarm of the plover, " Did he do it, did he do it?" is heard long after the rest of the feathered race are at rest.

Night in the Forest. Then the voices of night come upon our ears. Elephants are heard trumpetting as they crash through the underwood, and at intervals sundry smothered roars and deep hoarse grumblings re-echo amongst the hollow arches of the forest, and tell us that its fiercest denizens have risen from their lairs in its innermost recesses, and are prowling about in search of prey.

Forest Lore. It is not the mere killing which affords the hunter pleasure, as he ranges the forest in the pursuit of game, for the ever-changing sylvan realm is beautiful under

every aspect. The varied hues and forms of the
different trees, each possessing its own distinctive
character, are so beautifully blended by Nature
as to set at naught all the imitations of Art.
Here a crowd of interesting objects may be
embraced at a glance, on every side forming
vignettes such as Turner loved to delineate.
Yes, my gentle reader, the forest has indescribable
charms which grow round the heart, but he must
live long with Nature who would understand her
mysterious signs, hidden ways, and ever-changing
face, or interpret the wild voices of the woods—
a language which none save the long-initiated
can read.

The Ever-   The hunter, after a long sojourn in
changing Face
of Nature.   .these solitudes, gets accustomed to
observe the minutest change; nothing escapes
his keen observation, and by degrees, with close
attention, he begins to trace the cause by the
effect, and to study the regular, harmonious, and
systematic laws of Nature. Then he never suffers
from lassitude, gets disheartened, or is cast down'

when alone in the forest, for he has within himself an exhaustible source of occupation which keeps his mind active, his thoughts engaged, and his faculties in constant exercise. To him every object has its attraction and importance, either elucidating some principle or affording instruction; and the more he learns the more his curiosity is stimulated, rather than wearied, until after a time he becomes almost independent of external circumstances, and loses all craving after the artificial excitement of the outer world. He finds "that there is society where none intrudes," or, as the great master-mind Shakspere says:

"Tongues in trees—books in the running brooks—
Sermons in stones—and good in everything."

Instinct of Animals. Besides the beauties of Nature that meet the hunter at every step, the observation of the instincts, character, and habits of different animals is one of the most entertaining occupations. In the place of improvable reason given to man, all animals are endowed with faculties which impel them to perform certain

actions and guide them in certain operations
which cannot be ascribed to their own mental
consciousness, for some of their works show an
acquaintance with scientific principles which
man has only discovered by long reflection.
By watching closely the inhabitants of the forest,
the hunter will be struck with the different
sagacious expedients by which they provide
themselves with food, construct their habitations,
or defend themselves against their natural
enemies: and he will find that the capabilities
of all animals are proportionate to their wants;
thus some have different senses more strongly
developed than others. Sometimes the different
ingenious means and artifices animals resort
to will almost induce the observer to suspect
that they are endowed with a certain amount
of reason; yet, on reflection, he must be convinced
that this cannot be, as the ant and the bee, which
are of a very inferior class in the scale of animals,
possess an instinct more highly developed than
any other. The various means animals will resort

to for self-preservation are very extraordinary:
one class will endeavour to crush their antagonist
with their ponderous bodies; a second charge,
making use of their horns; a third employ their
paws and teeth, being gifted with immense mus-
cular strength; a fourth being protected by their
hides, roll themselves up in a ball; a fifth inject
subtle poison from hollow fangs; a sixth sting;
a seventh eject from their bodies a volatile fœtid
liquor offensive in the highest degree, or exhale
disagreeable and penetrating odours; an eighth
outstrip their pursuers by superior swiftness, fly,
climb out of the way, or creep into the earth; a
ninth counterfeit death on the presence of danger;
whilst others, again, have such extraordinary
vitality that dislocated portions grow and become
new animals.

Variety of
Characters.
The characters of different animals
vary extremely: some are naturally of
a savage and vindictive disposition; for instance,
the tiger's thirst for blood is insatiable, whereas
the lion does not attack his prey except from the

cravings of hunger; some are constitutionally brave, as the boar, buffalo, and bear; whilst others, such as the hyena and most of the feline class, are cowardly. Some are pugnacious, as the rhinoceros, jungle-cock, and spider; and others harmless by nature, and peacefully inclined, as the elephant and deer, except when excited by jealousy. Some are naturally solitary, only seeking each other during "the season of love," which comprises all the rapacious order of beasts or birds; others live in families, as the elephant; or in herds, as bison, deer, and antelope. Some associate only for the purposes of hunting, as wolves, jackals, wild dogs, and vultures; or previous to migrating, as swallows, snipe, and woodcock; whilst others live permanently together, as monkeys, parrots, rabbits, crows, pigeons, prairie dogs, and the society bird.* In some animals

---

* In Central Africa, I have come across the habitations of the society birds, which at first sight I imagined to have been constructed by man; for they live in hundreds together in a kind of mud and thatch-house, impervious to wet, having

memory and attachment to mankind are more strongly implanted by Nature than in others, more particularly in the dog, horse, and elephant.

The Language of Animals. The hunter may gain fresh insight into the nature and character of animals, by their cries under different circumstances which express their various desires and emotions, as all have certain calls and utter peculiar sounds denoting pleasure, sorrow, maternal affection, connubial attachment, anger, rage, alarm, and fear. In former days there were men who professed to understand the songs of birds; and often as I have listened to the merry songsters of the wood, or to the exquisitely plaintive melody of the turtle-dove as he wooed his bride, I have thought that it was quite possible to learn much of their language by watching their actions, and paying attention to the manifold accents of their

---

long streets, with lines of nests on each side at regular distances, from each other. The tree selected is generally the smooth-barked acacia.

notes—now low, soft, and long drawn out, now shrill, disjointed, and harsh.

These studies of Nature are the hunter's recreations, and he feels pleasure proportionate as he understands them. Her laws are ever the same, ever changeless, ever perfect. Truth is ever before him, and there are no imperfections in the models of his study—for Nature is ever young.

The Breathings of Nature. Yet there are mysterious natural phenomena met with in the dense forest, for which even the long-initiated hunter cannot account. I allude to those indescribable but peculiarly soothing and melodious sounds that issue from every side, and seem to make the very stillness palpable. My mentor, Walter M——, who, besides being the keenest sportsman was also the most skilled in woodcraft, and all knowledge appertaining to the forest that India ever produced, used to term these nameless sounds the "breathings of Nature;" and often, when watching for game in places far away from the haunts of man, have we listened, hour after hour, endeavouring to account for each of the various noises as they caught the ear.

Weird Music. The faint, soothing tones and humming sounds with which the forest is resonant at certain times are doubtlessly occasioned by the countless variety of insects that inhabit it; but sometimes when alone, even in broad daylight, the hunter will find strange emotions arise, and feel startled for the moment at the almost supernatural tone of the voices of the wild woods—for the unknown is always fearful, until habit has familiarised us with its presence; and when alone in those solitudes, man is deprived of that false courage that is engendered by the presence of his fellow-man.

Sometimes the hunter will hear resounding through these wilds, strange sounds like bursts of fiendish laughter, or long, protracted moanings, as if some human being was suffering in extreme agony; and by instinct he will cock his rifle and peer through the subdued light, and quickly flitting shadows, fully expecting to meet more than an earthly antagonist; but after a moment's reflection, he will lay down his trusty weapon with a smile at his own excitability, knowing that the strange sounds he has heard either proceeded from some prowling hyena, or were caused by the wind sweeping through the giant trees and rocky gorges. Again, sometimes, when on trail, he will fancy that he hears "floating sounds," like passing wings, and a hum like murmuring of voices in the air, and will stop and listen intently, fearing to move lest he should break the spell, when in reality it was only the creaking of boughs, bamboos rubbing against each other, or the foliage overhead being stirred by a gentle breeze.

A Hunter's Lullaby. Many a time in the still night, as he lays down to rest after the fatigues of the day, under some mighty patriarch of the forest, he will hear the wind sighing his lullaby among the distant hills, slow, sad, and melancholy. I remember in 1855, when crossing a lofty range of mountains in Circassia, that I was very much surprised, and my people frightened, at hearing low musical breathings, like the tones of an Æolian harp, evidently issuing from the side of the mountain. My followers called it "devil's music," and said that it prognosticated evil; but I believe that it was caused by strong currents of air passing swiftly over the numerous caverns and crevasses, although Humboldt attributes this natural phenomenon, which he also experienced, to parts of the ground being unequally heated.

Such is the forest-ranger's home, and he who has passed any length of time amid similar scenes will ever in his heart long to return to them, for no music is so sweet in his ears as "the voices of the wild woods."

Rousseau, the eloquent French author, in his "Confessions," says : "Never did a *level* country, however beautiful it might be, seem beautiful in my eyes. I must have cataracts, rocks, pines, dark forests, and rugged pathways, with steep precipices that make one shudder to behold." I cannot say that I entirely agree with him, for notwithstanding that I have wandered through all the wildest scenes of the Himalaya, my heart clings to the remembrance of the varied beauties of our English landscapes, where fields of waving golden corn, green meadows, woods, and gentle meandering rivers, alternate. There is a certain charm in such scenes that has an indescribable attraction to every traveller of the Anglo-Saxon race. He feels that it pertains of *home*—of the land of his fathers; with which no other spot on earth can compare. Yet there cannot be a doubt of the influence of mountain scenery upon the mind, and there is a spell in its contemplation that never palls. Here the wanderer's feet are rarely weary, his knapsack never heavy.

Mountain Life.   There is something invigorating in the pure bracing air of the higher altitudes that appears to revive the spirits after a lengthened sojourn amongst the dwellers of cities, and the change has a beneficial effect upon the body as well as upon the mind. Here one appears to inhale health at every respiration; the appetite improves, digestion becomes easy, physical force and elasticity of limb increases, and fallen degeneration changes to firm muscle, whilst a sense of exultation thrills through the whole frame; melancholy gives place to cheerfulness, and the mind feels relieved from all depressing influence of care and anxiety for the future. A life amid civilised society may seem to run smoothly, but "there's a skeleton in every house," and beneath are ever hidden strange things that occasion heart-aches, although they may never rise to the surface.

The wildness of a comparatively savage life is free from many of these troubles and disquietudes; and perfect freedom of action, even if it loses somewhat of refinement, gains much in liberty and the comforts of self-independence.

Mountain life has delights peculiarly its own, there is a mysterious charm in these elevated regions that is never felt on the plains, and the further the wanderer goes from the haunts of man, the stronger become those exhilarating sensations which fill the heart with gladness, and nerve the body with energy to put forth its strength. He who lives constantly with Nature, watching and studying all her changing moods, feels that he has a world within himself, that no adverse fortune can sweep away.

It has ever seemed to me that, amidst the mountains, the pulse of Nature beats stronger and more palpably than upon the plains ; here, everything discovers more life and energy, and speaks more emphatically of the infinite power of the Ruler of the Universe. The stream that meanders slowly through the plains, dashes impetuously down its mountain course ; and even man (unless education and society changes him) much resembles the soil from which he springs.

The Moun-
taineer.
To a certain extent, the mountaineer bears the stamp of Nature
upon him; for, like the mountain torrent, his
movements are quick; like the sudden changes
in the atmosphere in which he dwells, his passions
are easily roused; like the oak which shades him,
he has a sturdy, bold and characteristic manner;
like the rock on which he stands, he is true and
faithful, and makes a firm friend; and the constant presence of danger and peril inures him to
the contemplation of death, and renders him
fearless and intrepid.

Mountaineers are conspicuous for their independent manner, manly bearing, and the absence
of all conventional manner.

The Highest
Altitudes.
Imagination cannot portray to the
mind the stupendous grandeur of the
highest altitudes—here the whole face of nature
bears the stamp of immortality—seasons never
change—unbroken winter ever reigns. Such
scenery no mortal can contemplate, and still

disbelieve in the existence of God, for the voice of Nature is irresistibly powerful, and the mysterious influence that reigns in these regions will inculcate a natural religion even in the mind of a savage, and impress upon him the consciousness of the infinite supremacy of an all-ruling Power.

THE END.

*Post Office Orders payab e
at Piccadilly Circus.*]
[APRIL 1874.]

A LIST OF BOOKS

PUBLISHED BY

CHATTO & WINDUS,

74 & 75, *PICCADILLY, LONDON, W.*

THE FAMOUS FRASER PORTRAITS.

MACLISE'S
GALLERY OF ILLUSTRIOUS LITERARY CHARACTERS.

With Notes by the late WILLIAM MAGINN, LL.D.

Edited, with copious Notes, by WILLIAM BATES, B.A., Professor of Classics in Queen's College, Birmingham. The volume contains the whole 83 SPLENDID AND MOST CHARACTERISTIC PORTRAITS, now first issued in a complete form. In demy 4to, over 400 pages, cloth gilt and gilt edges, 31s. 6d.

"Most interesting."—*Saturday Review.*
"Not possible to imagine a more elegant addition to a drawing-room table."—*Fun.*
"One of the most interesting volumes of this year's literature."—*Times.*
"Deserves a place on every drawing-room table, and may not unfitly be removed from the drawing-room to the library."—*Spectator.*

74 & 75, *PICCADILLY, LONDON, W.*

B

THE NATIONAL GALLERY.

A Selection from its Pictures, by CLAUDE, REMBRANDT, CUYP, Sir DAVID WILKIE, CORREGGIO, GAINSBOROUGH, CANALETTI, VANDYCK, PAUL VERONESE, CARACCI, RUBENS, N. and G. POUSSIN, and other great Masters. Engraved by GEORGE DOO, JOHN BURNET, WILLIAM FINDEN, JOHN and HENRY LE KEUX, JOHN PYE, WALTER BROMLEY, and others. With descriptive Text. A NEW EDITION, from the original Plates, in Columbier 4to, cloth extra, gilt and gilt edges, 31s. 6d.   [*Nearly ready.*

WORKS OF JAMES GILLRAY, CARICATURIST.

With the Story of his Life and Times, and full and Anecdotal Descriptions of his Engravings. Edited by THOS. WRIGHT, Esq., M.A., F.S.A. Illustrated with 83 full-page Plates, and very numerous Wood Engravings. Demy 4to, 600 pages, cloth extra, 31s. 6d.

"The work is well done. A handsome volume, produced regardless of expense."
—*Standard.*

"The publishers have done good service in bringing so much that is full of humour and of historical interest within the reach of a large class."—*Saturday Review.*

"One of the most amusing and valuable illustrations of the social and polished life of that generation which it is possible to conceive."—*Spectator.*

BEAUTIFUL PICTURES BY BRITISH ARTISTS.

A Gathering of Favourites from our Picture Galleries, 1800—1870. By WILKIE, CONSTABLE, J. M. W. TURNER, MULREADY, Sir EDWIN LANDSEER, MACLISE, LESLIE, E. M. WARD, FRITH, Sir JOHN GILBERT, ANSDELL, MARCUS STONE, Sir NOEL PATON, EYRE CROWE, FAED, MADOX BROWN. All Engraved in the highest style of Art. With Notices of the Artists by SYDNEY ARMYTAGE, M.A. A New Edition. Imperial 4to, cloth gilt and gilt edges, 21s.

COURT BEAUTIES OF THE REIGN OF CHARLES II.

From the Originals in the Royal Gallery at Windsor, by Sir PETER LELY. Engraved in the highest style of art by THOMSON, WRIGHT, SCRIVEN, B. HOLL, WAGSTAFF, and T. A. DEANE. With Memoirs by Mrs. JAMESON, Author of "Legends of the Madonna." New and sumptuous "Presentation Edition." Imp. 4to, cloth gilt and gilt edges, 21s.

"This truly beautiful and splendid production is equally a gem among the Fine Arts and in Literature."—*Quarterly Review.*

MATT MORGAN'S DESIGNS.

THE AMERICAN WAR:

CARTOONS by MATT MORGAN and other Artists, illustrative of the late Great Civil War in America. Now first collected, with Explanatory Text. Demy 4to, illustrated boards, 7s. 6d.

COMPANION TO THE "HISTORY OF SIGNBOARDS."

Advertising, A History of, from the

Earliest Times. Illustrated by Anecdotes, Curious Specimens, Biographical Notes, and Examples of Successful Advertisers. By HENRY SAMPSON. Crown 8vo, with Frontispiece and numerous Illustrations, coloured and plain, cloth extra, 7s. 6d. [*In preparation.*

Anacreon. Illustrated by

the Exquisite Designs of GIRODET. Translated by THOMAS MOORE. Bound in Etruscan gold and blue, 12s. 6d.

*** *A beautiful and captivating volume. The well-known Paris house, Firmin Didot, a few years since produced a miniature edition of these exquisite designs by photography, and sold a large number at £2 per copy. The Designs have been universally admired by both artists and poets.*

The Art of Amusing.

A Collection of Graceful Arts, Games, Tricks, Puzzles, and Charades, intended to amuse everybody, and enable all to amuse everybody else. By FRANK BELLEW. With nearly 300 Illustrations. Crown 8vo, 4s. 6d.

*** *One of the most entertaining handbooks of amusements ever published.*

Awful Crammers.

A New American Joke Book. Edited by TITUS A. BRICK, Author of "Shaving 'Them." Fcap. 8vo, with numerous curious Illustrations, 1s.

74 & 75, PICCADILLY, LONDON, W.

Army Lists of the Roundheads and

Cavaliers in the Civil War, 1642. SECOND EDITION, considerably Enlarged and Corrected. Edited, with Notes, by EDWARD PEACOCK, F.S.A. 4to, half-Roxburghe, 7s. 6d.   [*Preparing.*

*** Very interesting to Antiquaries and Genealogists.*

Babies and Ladders:

Essays on Things in General. By EMMANUEL KINK. Fcap. 8vo, with numerous Vignettes by W. S. GILBERT and others. 1s.

Bayard Taylor's Di-

versions of the Echo Club. A Delightful Volume of Refined Literary Humour. In 16mo, paper cover, with Portrait of the Author, 1s. 6d. ; cloth extra, 2s.

UNIFORM WITH MR. RUSKIN'S EDITION OF "GRIMM."

Bechstein's As Pretty as Seven, and

other Popular German Stories. Collected by LUDWIG BECHSTEIN. With Additional Tales by the Brothers GRIMM. 100 Illustrations by RICHTER. Small 4to, green and gold, 6s. 6d. ; gilt edges, 7s. 6d.

*** One of the most delightful books for children ever published. It is, in every way, a Companion to the German Stories of the Brothers Grimm. The quaint simplicity of Richter's engravings will charm every lover of legendary lore.*

The Biglow Papers. By JAMES RUSSELL

LOWELL. The Best Edition, with full Glossary, of these extraordinary Verses. Fcap. 8vo, illustrated cover, 1s.

ARTEMUS WARD'S WORKS.

Artemus Ward,

Complete. The Works of CHARLES FARRER BROWNE, better known as ARTEMUS WARD, now first collected. Crown 8vo, with fine Portrait, facsimile of handwriting, &c., 540 pages, cloth neat, 7s. 6d.

** Comprises all that the humourist has written in England or America. Admirers of Artemus Ward will be glad to possess his writings in a complete form.

Artemus Ward's

Lecture at the Egyptian Hall, with the Panorama. Edited by the late T. W. ROBERTSON, Author of "Caste," &c., and E. P. HINGSTON. Small 4to, exquisitely printed, bound in green and gold, with NUMEROUS TINTED ILLUSTRATIONS, 6s.

Artemus Ward : his Book. With Notes

and Introduction by the Editor of the "Biglow Papers." One of the wittiest books published for many years. Fcap, 8vo, illustrated cover, 1s.

The *Saturday Review* says:—"The author combines the powers of Thackeray with those of Albert Smith. The salt is rubbed in by a native hand—one which has the gift of tickling."

Artemus Ward : his Travels among

the Mormons and on the Rampage. Edited by E. P. HINGSTON, the Agent and Companion of A. WARD whilst "on the Rampage." New Edition, price 1s.

** Some of Artemus's most mirth-provoking papers are to be found in this book. The chapters on the Mormons will unbend the sternest countenance. As bits of fun they are IMMENSE!

Artemus Ward's Letters to "Punch,"

Among the Witches, and other Sketches. Cheap Popular Edition. Fcap. 8vo, in illustrated cover, 1s.; or, 16mo, bound in cloth extra, 2s.

** The volume contains, in addition, some quaint and humorous compositions which were found upon the author's table after his decease.

Artemus Ward among the Fenians :

with the Showman's Experiences of Life at Washington, and Military Ardour at Baldinsville. Toned paper, price 6d.

74 & 75, PICCADILLY, LONDON, W.

UNIFORM WITH OUR "RABELAIS."

Boccaccio's Decameron;

or, Ten Days' Entertainment. Now fully
translated into English, with Introduction by THOMAS WRIGHT, Esq., M.A.,
F.S.A.   Crown 8vo, with the BEAUTI-
FUL ENGRAVINGS by STOTHARD which
adorned Pickering's fine Edition, published at £2 12s. 6d. This New
Edition is only 7s. 6d.

Booksellers, A History of.   A Work

giving full Accounts of the Great Publishing Houses and their
Founders, both in London and the Provinces, the History of
their Rise and Progress, and of their greatest Works. By HARRY
CURWEN.   Crown 8vo, over 500 pages, with frontispiece and numerous Portraits and Illustrations, cloth extra, 7s. 6d.

HEADPIECE USED BY WILLIAM CAXTON.

"*In these days, ten ordinary Histories of Kings and Courtiers were well exchanged against the te eth part of one good History of Booksellers.*"—THOMAS
CARLYLE.

Book of Hall-Marks ; or, Manual of

Reference for the Goldsmith and Silversmith. By ALFRED LUT-
SCHAUNIG, Manager of the Liverpool Assay Office. Crown 8vo, with
46 Plates of the Hall-Marks of the different Assay Towns of the
United Kingdom, as now stamped on Plate and Jewellery, 7s. 6d.

*** *This work gives practical methods for testing the quality of gold and silver.
It was compiled by the author for his own use, and as a Supplement to "Chaffers."*

74 & 75, PICCADILLY, LONDON, W.

BRET HARTE'S WORKS.

Widely known for their Exquisite Pathos and Delightful Humour.

Bret Harte's Complete Works, in Prose and Poetry. Now First Collected. With Introductory Essay by J. M. BELLEW, Portrait of the Author, and 50 Illustrations. Crown 8vo, 650 pages, cloth extra, 7s. 6d.

Bret Harte's Luck of Roaring Camp, and other Stories. Fcap. 8vo, illustrated cover, 1s.

Bret Harte's That Heathen Chinee, and other Humorous Poems. Fcap. 8vo, illustrated cover, 1s. 6d.

Bret Harte's Sensation Novels Condensed. Fcap. 8vo, illustrated cover, 1s. 6d.

** A most enjoyable book, only surpassed, in its special class, by Thackeray's Burlesque Novels.

Bret Harte's Lothaw ; or, The Adventures of a Young Gentleman in Search of a Religion. By Mr. BENJAMINS *(Bret Harte)*. Price 6d. Curiously Illustrated.

Bret Harte's East and West. Fcap. 8vo, illustrated cover, 1s.

Bret Harte's Stories of the Sierras, and other Sketches. With a Wild Story of Western Life by JOAQUIN MILLER, Author of "Songs of the Sierras." Illustrated cover, 1s.

Booth's Epigrams : Ancient and Modern, Humorous, Witty, Satirical, Moral, and Panegyrical. Edited by the Rev. JOHN BOOTH, B.A. A New Edition. Pott 8vo, cloth gilt, 6s.

Brewster's (Sir David) More Worlds

than One, the Creed of the Philosopher and the Hope of the Christian. A NEW EDITION, in small crown 8vo, cloth, extra gilt, with full-page Astronomical Plates, uniform with Faraday's "Chemical History of a Candle." 4s. 6d. [*Nearly ready.*]

Brewster's (Sir David) Martyrs of

Science. A NEW EDITION, in small crown 8vo, cloth, extra gilt, with full-page Portraits, uniform with Faraday's "Various Forces of Nature." 4s. 6d. [*Nearly ready.*]

NEW BOOK FOR BOYS.

The Conquest of the Sea: A History

of Divers and Diving, from the Earliest Times to the Present Day. By HENRY SIEBE. Profusely Illustrated with fine Wood Engravings. Small crown 8vo, cloth extra, 4s. 6d.

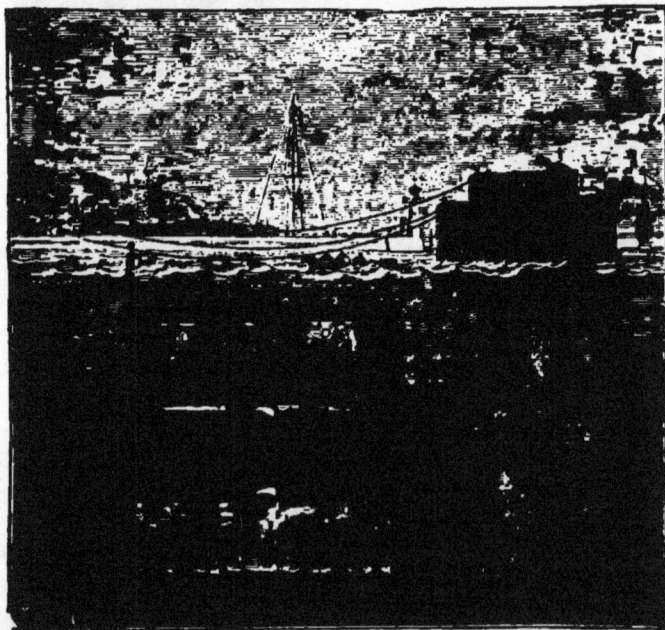

"We have perused this volume, full of quaint information, with delight. Mr. Siebe has bestowed much pains on his work ; he writes with enthusiasm and fulness of knowledge."—*Echo.*

" Really interesting alike to youths and to grown-up people."—*Scotsman.*

"Equally interesting to the general and to the scientific reader."—*Morning Advertiser.*

Bright's (Rt. Hon. J., M.P.) Speeches

on Public Affairs of the last Twenty Years. Collated with the best Public Reports. Royal 16mo, 370 pages, cloth extra, 1s.

✱ *A book of special interest at the present time, and wonderfully cheap.*

COLMAN'S HUMOROUS WORKS.

Broad Grins. My Nightgown and Slippers,

and other Humorous Works, Prose and Poetical, of GEORGE COL-
MAN the Younger. Now first collected, with Life and Anecdotes of
the Author, by GEORGE B. BUCKSTONE. Crown 8vo, 500 pp.,7s. 6d.

✱ *Admirers of genuine English wit and humour will be delighted with this
edition of George Colman's humorous works. As a wit, he has had no equal in
our time; and a man with a tithe of his ability could, at the present day, make
the fortune of any of our comic journals.*

Carlyle (T.) on the Choice of Books.

With New Life and Anecdotes. Brown cloth, UNIFORM WITH THE
2s. EDITION OF HIS WORKS, 1s. 6d. ; paper cover, 1s.

Celebrated Claim-

ants, Ancient and Modern. Being
the Histories of all the most celebrated Pretenders and Claimants
during the last 600 years. Fcap.
8vo, 300 pages, illustrated boards,
2s.

✱ *This book is
presented to the pub-
lic at a time when
popular attention is
attracted to the sub-
ject of which it
treats; but it is in-
tended much less to
gratify a temporary
curiosity than to fill
an empty page in
our literature. In
our own and in other
countries Claimants
have been by no
means rare, and the
author has spared
no research to render
his work as perfect
as possible, and to
supply a reliable
history of those cases which are entitled to rank as* causes célèbres. *The book
is put forward in the hope that, while it may serve to amuse the hasty reader in
a leisure hour, it may also be deemed worthy of a modest resting-place in the
libraries of those who like to watch the march of events, and who have the prudent
habit, when information is found, of preserving a note of it.*

---

74 & 75, PICCADILLY, LONDON, W.

NEW AND IMPORTANT WORK.

The Cyclopædia of Costume; or, A

Dictionary of Dress, Regal, Ecclesiastical, Civil, and Military, from the Earliest Period in England to the reign of George the Third. Including Notices of Contemporaneous Fashions on the Continent, and preceded by a General History of the Costume of the Principal Countries of Europe. By J. R. PLANCHÉ, F.S.A., Somerset Herald.

This work will be published in Twenty-four Monthly Parts, quarto, at Five Shillings, profusely illustrated by Plates and Wood Engravings; with each Part will also be issued a splendid Coloured Plate, from an original Painting or Illumination, of Royal and Noble Personages, and National Costume, both foreign and domestic. The First Part is just ready.

IN collecting materials for a History of Costume of more importance than the little handbook which has met with so much favour as an elementary work, I was not only made aware of my own deficiencies, but surprised to find how much more vague are the explanations, and contradictory the statements, of our best authorities, than they appeared to me, when, in the plenitude of my ignorance, I rushed upon almost untrodden ground, and felt bewildered by the mass of unsifted evidence and unhesitating assertion which met my eyes at every turn.

During the forty years which have elapsed since the publication of the first edition of my "History of British Costume" in the "Library of Entertaining Knowledge," archæological investigation has received such an impetus by the establishment of metropolitan and provincial peripatetic antiquarian societies, that a flood of light has been poured upon us, by which we are enabled to re-examine our opinions and discover reasons to doubt, if we cannot find facts to authenticate.

That the former greatly preponderate is a grievous acknowledgment to make after assiduously devoting the leisure of half my life to the pursuit of information on this, to me, most fascinating subject. It is some consolation, however, to feel that where I cannot instruct, I shall certainly not mislead, and that the reader will find, under each head, all that is known to, or suggested by, the most competent writers I am acquainted with, either here or on the Continent.

That this work appears in a glossarial form arises from the desire of many artists, who have expressed to me the difficulty they constantly meet with in their endeavours to ascertain the complete form of a garment, or the exact mode of fastening a piece of armour, or buckling of a belt, from their study of a sepulchral effigy or a figure in an illumination, the attitude of the personages represented, or the disposition of other portions of their attire, effectually preventing the requisite examination. The books supplying any such information are very few, and the best confined to armour or ecclesiastical costume. The only English publication of the kind required, that I am aware of, is the late Mr. Fairholt's "Costume in England" (8vo, London, 1846), the last two hundred pages of which contain a glossary, the most valuable portion whereof are the quotations from old plays, mediæval romances, and satirical ballads, containing allusions to various articles of attire in fashion at the time of their composition. Twenty-eight years have expired since that book appeared, and it has been thought that a more comprehensive work on the subject than has yet issued from the English press, combining the pith of the information of many costly foreign publications, and, in its illustrations, keeping in view the special requirement of the artist, to which I have alluded, would be, in these days of educational progress and critical inquiry, a welcome addition to the library of an English gentleman.   J. R. PLANCHÉ.

Christmas Carols and Ballads. Selected

and Edited by Joshua Sylvester. A New Edition, beautifully printed and bound in cloth, extra gilt, gilt edges, 3*s.* 6*d.*

Clerical Anecdotes and Pulpit Eccen-

tricities. Square 16mo, illustrated wrapper, 1*s.* 4*d.*; cloth neat, 1*s.* 10*d.*

The Country of the Dwarfs. By Paul

du Chaillu. Fcap. 8vo, full-page Engravings, fancy wrapper, 1*s.*

Cruikshank's Comic Almanack.

Complete in Two Series: the First from 1835 to 1843; the Second from 1844 to 1853. A Gathering of the Best Humour of Thackeray, Hood, Mayhew, Albert Smith, A'Beckett, Robert Brough, &c. With 2,000 Woodcuts and Steel Engravings by Cruikshank, Hine, Landells, &c. Crown 8vo, cloth gilt, two very thick volumes, 15*s.*; or, separately, 7*s.* 6*d.* per volume.

APPROACH OF BLUCHER: INTREPID ADVANCE OF THE FIRST FOOT.

*** The "Comic Almanacks" of George Cruikshank have long been regarded by admirers of this inimitable artist as among his finest, most characteristic productions. Extending over a period of nineteen years, from 1835 to 1853, inclusive, they embrace the best period of his artistic career, and show the varied excellences of his marvellous power. The late Mr. Tilt, of Fleet Street, first conceived the idea of the "Comic Almanack," and at various times there were engaged upon it such writers as Thackeray, Albert Smith, the Brothers Mayhew, the late Robert Brough, Gilbert A'Beckett, and, it has been asserted, Tom Hood the elder. Thackeray's stories of "Stubbs' Calendar; or, The Fatal Boots," which subsequently appeared as "Stubbs' Diary;" and "Barber Cox; or, The Cutting of His Comb," formed the leading attractions in the numbers for 1839 and 1840.

74 & 75, PICCADILLY, LONDON, W.

THE BEST GUIDE TO HERALDRY.

Cussans' Handbook of

Heraldry; with Instructions for Tracing Pedigrees and Deciphering Ancient MSS.; also, Rules for the Appointment of Liveries, &c., &c. By JOHN E. CUSSANS. Illustrated with 360 Plates and Woodcuts. Crown 8vo, cloth extra, gilt and emblazoned, 7s. 6d.

** *This volume, beautifully printed on toned paper, contains not only the ordinary matter to be found in the best books on the science of Armory, but several other subjects hitherto unnoticed. Amongst these may be mentioned:*—1. DIRECTIONS FOR TRACING PEDIGREES. 2. DECIPHERING ANCIENT MSS., ILLUSTRATED BY ALPHABETS AND FACSIMILES. 3. THE APPOINTMENT OF LIVERIES. 4. CONTINENTAL AND AMERICAN HERALDRY, &c.

VERY IMPORTANT COUNTY HISTORY.

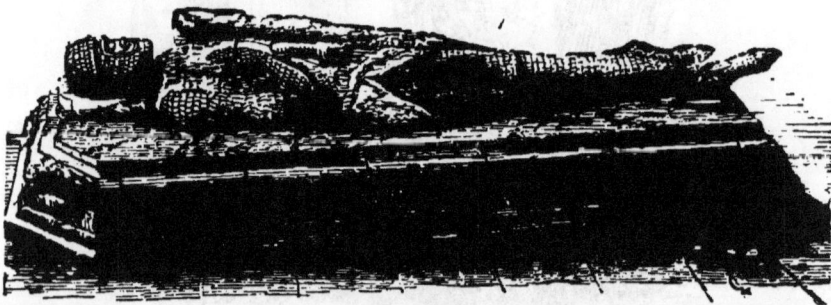

Cussans' History of Hertfordshire.

A County History, got up in a very superior manner, and ranging with the finest works of its class. By JOHN E. CUSSANS. Illustrated with full-page Plates on Copper and Stone, and a profusion of small Woodcuts. Parts I. to VI. are now ready, price 21s. each.

** *An entirely new History of this important County, great attention being given to all matters pertaining to the Family History of the locality.*

The Danbury Newsman. A Brief but

Comprehensive Record of the Doings of a Remarkable People, under more Remarkable Circumstances, and Chronicled in a most Remarkable Manner. By JAMES M. BAILEY. Uniform with Twain's " Screamers." Fcap. 8vo, illustrated cover, 1s.

"A real American humourist."—*Figaro.*

UNIFORM WITH THE "CHARLES DICKENS EDITION."

Dickens : The Story

of his Life. By THEODORE TAYLOR, Author of the "Life of Thackeray." Uniform with the "Charles Dickens Edition" of his Works, and forming a Supplementary Volume to that Issue. Crown 8vo, crimson cloth, 3s. 6d.

"Anecdotes seem to have poured in upon the author from all quarters. . . Turn where we will through these 370 pleasant pages, something worth reading is sure to meet the eye."—*The Standard.*

Also Published :

THE "BEST EDITION" of the above Work, illustrated by Photographic Frontispiece of "Dickens as Captain Bobadil," Portraits, Facsimiles, &c. Crown 8vo, cloth extra, 7s. 6d.

THE "CHEAP EDITION," in 16mo, paper wrapper, with Frontispiece and Vignette, 2s.

UNIFORM WITH THE "CHARLES DICKENS EDITION."

Dickens' Speeches, Social and Literary,

now first collected. Uniform with, and forming a Supplementary Volume to, the "CHARLES DICKENS EDITION." Crown 8vo, crimson cloth, 3s. 6d.

"His speeches are as good as any of his printed writings."—*The Times.*

Also Published:

THE "BEST EDITION," in crown 8vo, with fine Portrait by Count D'ORSAY, cloth extra, 7s. 6d.

THE "CHEAP EDITION," in 16mo, paper wrapper, 2s.

Dickens' Life and Speeches, One Volume, 16mo, cloth, 2s. 6d.

BALZAC'S CONTES DROLATIQUES.

Droll Sto-ries, collected from the Abbeys of Touraine.

NOW FIRST TRANSLATED INTO ENGLISH, COMPLETE AND UNABRIDGED.

With the whole 425 Marvellous, Extravagant, and Fantastic Illustrations by GUSTAVE DORÉ. Beautifully printed, in 8vo, cloth extra, gilt, gilt top, *12s. 6d.*

A few copies of the FRENCH ORIGINAL are still on sale, bound half-Roxburghe, gilt top—a very handsome book—price *12s. 6d.*

The Derby Day. A Sporting Novel of intense interest. Fcap. 8vo, illustrated cover, *1s.*

Disraeli's (Rt. Hon. B.) Speeches on the Conservative Policy of the last Thirty Years, including the Speech at the Literary Fund Dinner, specially revised by the Author. Royal 16mo, paper cover, with Portrait, *1s. 4d.* ; in cloth, *1s. 10d.*

D'Urfey's ("Tom") Wit and Mirth;

or, PILLS TO PURGE MELANCHOLY: Being a Collection of the best Merry Ballads and Songs, Old and New. Fitted to all Humours, having each their proper Tune for either Voice or Instrument: most of the Songs being new set. London: Printed by W. Pearson, for J. Tonson, at Shakespeare's Head, over-against Catherine Street in the Strand, 1719.

An exact and beautiful reprint of this much-prized work, with the Music to the Songs, just as in the rare original. In 6 vols., large fcap. 8vo, antique boards, edges uncut, beautifully printed on laid paper, made expressly for the work, price £3 3s.

. *The PILLS TO PURGE MELANCHOLY have now retained their celebrity for a century and a half. The difficulty of obtaining a copy has of late years raised sets to a fabulous price, and has made even odd volumes costly. Considering the classical reputation which the book has thus obtained, and its very high interest as illustrative of the manners, customs, and amusements of English life during the half century following the Restoration, no apology is needed for placing such a work more within the reach of general readers and students by re-issuing it for the first time since its original appearance, and at about a tithe of the price for which the old edition could now be obtained.*

For drinking-songs and love-songs, sprightly ballads, merry stories, and political squibs, there are none to surpass these in the language. In improvising such pieces, and in singing them, D'URFEY was perhaps never equalled, except in our own century by THEODORE HOOK. The sallies of his wit amused and delighted three successive English sovereigns; and while his plays are forgotten, his songs and ballads still retain the light abandon and joyous freshness that recommended them to the wits and beaux of Queen Anne's days. Nor can the warm and affectionate eulogy of Steele and Addison be forgotten, and D'URFEY may now take his place on the bookshelves of the curious, side by side with the other worthies of his age.

The Earthward Pilgrimage, from the

Next World to that which now is. By MONCURE D. CONWAY. Crown 8vo, beautifully printed and bound, 7s. 6d.

Mrs. Ellis's Mothers of Great Men.

A New Edition of this well-known Work, with Illustrations by VALENTINE W. BROMLEY and others. Crown 8vo, cloth gilt, over 500 pages, 6s.

Emanuel on Diamonds and Precious

Stones; Their History, Value, and Properties; with Simple Tests for ascertaining their Reality. By HARRY EMANUEL, F.R.G.S. With numerous Illustrations, Tinted and Plain. A New Edition, Crown 8vo, cloth extra, gilt, 6s.

Edgar Allan Poe's Prose and Poetical

Works; including Additional Tales and the fine Essays by this

POE'S COTTAGE AT FORDHAM.

great Genius, now FIRST PUBLISHED IN THIS COUNTRY. With a Translation of CHARLES BAUDELAIRE'S "Essay on Poe." 750 pages, crown 8vo, fine Portrait and Illustrations, cloth extra, 7s.6d.

The English Rogue, described in the

Life of MERITON LATROON, and other Extravagants, comprehending the most Eminent Cheats of both Sexes. By RICHARD HEAD and FRANCIS KIRKMAN. A facsimile reprint of the rare Original Edition (1665-1672), with a Frontispiece and Portraits of the Authors. In 4 Volumes, large foolscap 8vo, beautifully printed on antique laid paper, made expressly, and bound in antique boards, 32s.; or LARGE-PAPER COPIES, 52s. [*Nearly ready.*

** This singularly entertaining work may be described as the first English novel, properly so called. The same air of reality pervades it as that which gives such a charm to the stories written by Defoe half a century later. The interest never flags for a moment, from the first chapter to the last.

As a picture of the manners of the period, two hundred years ago, in England, among the various grades of society through which the hero passes in the course of his extraordinary adventures, and among gipsies, beggars, thieves, &c., the book is invaluable to students.

The earlier portion of the book was considerably altered in later editions by Francis Kirkman, While preserving all the additions made by that writer, most of the omitted passages (sometimes among the most characteristic in the book) have been restored from the earliest edition, which is of the very greatest rarity, most of the copies having been destroyed, the year after its publication, in the Great Fire of London.

The later edition and the Second Part are of almost equal rarity. Owing to its wonderful run of popularity, the book has been so well read and well thumbed, that perfect copies are very seldom to be met with, and are then only to be obtained at an extravagantly high price. The present reprint may therefore be useful and acceptable to students of Early English Literature.

Our English Surnames: Their Sources
and Significations. By CHARLES WAREING BARDSLEY, M.A.
Crown 8vo, about 600 pages, cloth extra, 9s.

. *A complete work, containing very much that is not to be found in Mr.
Lower's well-known volume. The chapters are arranged under the following
heads:*—1. BAPTISMAL OR PERSONAL NAMES; 2. LOCAL SURNAMES; 3. OFFICIAL
SURNAMES; 4. OCCUPATIVE SURNAMES; 5. SOBRIQUET SURNAMES, OR NICKNAMES.

EARLY NEWS SHEET.

The Russian Invasion of Poland in
1563. (Memorabilis et perinde stupenda de crudeli Moscovitarum
Expeditione Narratio, e Germanico in Latinum conversa.) An exact
facsimile of a contemporary account in Latin, published at Douay,
together with an Introduction and Historical Notes and a full Translation. Only 100 copies printed. Large fcap. 8vo, an exact facsimile on antique paper, hardly distinguishable from the original,
half-Roxburghe, price 7s. 6d.

The Englishman's House, from a Cot-
tage to a Mansion. A Practical Guide to Members of Building
Societies, and all interested in Selecting or Building a House. By
C. J. RICHARDSON, Architect, Author of "Old English Mansions,"
&c. Second Edition, Corrected and Enlarged, with nearly 600
Illustrations. Crown 8vo, 550 pages, cloth, 7s. 6d.

. *This Work might not inappropriately be termed "A Book of Houses." It
gives every variety of house, from a workman's cottage to a nobleman's palace.
The book is intended to supply a want long felt, viz., a plain, non-technical
account of every style of house, with the cost and manner of building.*

74 & 75, *PICCADILLY, LONDON, W.*

Faraday's Chemical History of a
Candle. Lectures delivered to a Juvenile Audience. A New Edition, edited by W. CROOKES, Esq., F.C.S., &c. Crown 8vo, cloth extra, with all the Original Illustrations, price 4s. 6d.

Faraday's Various Forces of Nature.
A New Edition, edited by W. CROOKES, Esq., F.C.S., &c. Crown 8vo, cloth extra, with all the Original Illustrations, price 4s. 6d.

FLAGELLATION AND THE FLAGELLANTS.

A History of the Rod in all Countries,
from the Earliest Period to the Present Time. By the Rev. W. COOPER, B.A. Second Edition, revised and corrected, with numerous Illustrations. Thick crown, 8vo, cloth extra, gilt, 12s. 6d.

The Fiend's Delight: A "Cold Collation"
of Atrocities. By DOD GRILE. New Edition, in illustrated wrapper, fcap. 8vo, 1s.

"A specimen of 'American Humour' as unlike that of all other American humourists, as the play of young human Merry-Andrews is unlike that of a young and energetic demon whose horns are well budded."—*New York Nation.*

The Finish to Life in and out of
London; or, The Final Adventures of Tom, Jerry, and Logic. By PIERCE EGAN. Royal 8vo, cloth extra, with Spirited Coloured Illustrations by CRUIKSHANK, 21s.

Fun for the Million:
A Gathering of Choice Wit and Humour, Good Things, and Sublime Nonsense, by DICKENS, JERROLD, SAM SLICK, CHAS. II. ROSS, HOOD, THEODORE HOOK, MARK TWAIN, BROUGH, COLMAN, TITUS A. BRICK, and a Host of other Humourists. With Pictures by MATT MORGAN, GILBERT, NAST, THOMPSON, CRUIKSHANK, Jun., BRUNTON, &c. In fcap. 4to, profusely illustrated, with picture wrapper, 1s.

WALK UP! WALK UP! AND SEE THE

Fools' Paradise ; with the Many Wonder-
ful Adventures there, as seen in the strange, surprising
PEEP-SHOW OF PROFESSOR WOLLEY COBBLE,
Raree Showman these Five-and-Twenty Years.
Crown 4to, with nearly 200 immensely funny Pictures, all beautifully
coloured, bound in extra cloth gilt, price 7s. 6d.

THE PROFESSOR'S LEETLE MUSIC LESSON.

A SECOND SERIES IS NOW READY, CALLED

Further Adventures in Fools' Paradise,
with the Many Wonderful Doings, as seen in the
PEEP-SHOW OF PROFESSOR WOLLEY COBBLE.
Crown 4to, with the Pictures beautifully Coloured, uniform with the
FIRST SERIES, in extra cloth gilt, price 7s. 6d.

THE OLD SHEKARRY.

The Forest and the Field : Life and
Adventure in Wild Africa. By the OLD SHEKARRY. With Eight
Illustrations. Crown 8vo, cloth extra, gilt, 6s.

*** The Author has endeavoured to record his impressions of some of the
grandest scenery in the world, as well as of the dreary swamps of the Eastern
coast of Equatorial Africa. It is a book of intense interest, especially for boys.*

Wrinkles ; or, Hints to Sportsmen and
Travellers upon Dress, Equipment, Armament, and Camp Life.
By the OLD SHEKARRY. A New Edition, with Illustrations. Small
Crown 8vo, cloth extra, gilt, 6s.

The Genial Showman; or, Show Life

in the New World. Adventures with Artemus Ward, and the Story of his Life. By E. P. HINGSTON. Third Edition. Crown 8vo, Illustrated by BRUNTON, cloth extra, 7s. 6d.

RUSKIN AND CRUIKSHANK.

German Popular Stories. Collected by

the Brothers GRIMM, and Translated by EDGAR TAYLOR. Edited by JOHN RUSKIN. With 22 Illustrations after the inimitable designs of GEORGE CRUIKSHANK. Both Series complete. Square crown 8vo, 6s. 6d.; gilt leaves, 7s. 6d.

*** These are the designs which Mr. Ruskin has praised so highly, placing them 'ar above all Cruikshank's other works of a similar character.*

Gesta Romanorum; or, Entertaining

Stories, invented by the Monks as a Fireside Recreation, and commonly applied in their Discourses from the Pulpit. A New Edition, with Introduction by THOMAS WRIGHT, Esq., M.A., F.S.A. Two vols. large fcap. 8vo, printed on fine ribbed paper, 18s.

Gladstone's (Rt. Hon. W. E.) Speeches

on Great Questions of the Day during the last Thirty Years. Collated with the best public reports. Royal 16mo, paper cover, 1s. 4d.; cloth extra, 1s. 10d.

VERS DE SOCIÉTÉ.

Golden Gleanings from Poets of the

Nineteenth Century: TENNYSON, BROWNING, SWINBURNE, ROSSETTI, JEAN INGELOW, HOOD, LYTTON, and very many others. Edited by H. CHOLMONDELEY-PENNELL, Author of "Puck on Pegasus." Beautifully printed, and bound in cloth, extra gilt, uniform with the "Golden Treasury of Thought." 7s. 6d. [*Nearly ready.*]

Golden Treasury of Thought. The Best

Encyclopædia of Quotations and Elegant Extracts, from Writers of all Times and all Countries, ever formed. Selected and Edited by THEODORE TAYLOR, Author of "Thackeray, the Humourist and Man of Letters," "Story of Charles Dickens' Life." Crown 8vo, very handsomely bound, cloth gilt, and gilt edges, 7s. 6d.

*** An attempt to put into the hands of the reader and student a more varied and complete collection of the best thoughts of the best authors than had before been made. It is not everybody who can get the original works from which the extracts are taken, while a book such as this is within the reach of all, and cannot be opened without finding something worth reading, and in most cases worth remembering.*

The Great Condé, and the Period of

the Fronde: An Historical Sketch. By WALTER FITZPATRICK. Second Edition, in 2 vols. 8vo, cloth extra, 15*s.*

"A very agreeable, trustworthy, and readable sketch of a famous man."—*Standard.*

"Mr. FitzPatrick has given us a history that is pleasant to read: his style is incisive and picturesque as well as fluent. . . . . . The work is well done, historically and morally."—*Tablet.*

"The sketches of the characters and careers of the extraordinary men and women who lived, intrigued, governed, or strove to govern, are admirable for their life-likeness."—*Morning Post.*

Greenwood's (James), Wilds of

London. With a Full Account of the Natives : being Descriptive Sketches, from the Personal Observations and Experiences of the Writer, of Remarkable Scenes, People, and Places in London. By JAMES GREENWOOD, the "Lambeth Casual." Crown 8vo, cloth, extra gilt, with Illustrations, 6*s.*   [*Preparing.*

Grose's Dictionary of the Vulgar

Tongue. 1785. A genuine unmutilated Reprint of the First Edition. Quarto, bound in half-Roxburghe, gilt top, price 8*s.*

*** *Only a small number of copies of this very vulgar, but very curious, book have been printed, for the Collectors of "Street Words" and Colloquialisms.*

COMPANION TO "THE SECRET OUT."

Hanky-Panky. A New and Wonderful

Book of Very Easy Tricks, Very Difficult Tricks, White Magic, Sleight of Hand ; in fact, all those startling Deceptions which the Great Wizards call "Hanky-Panky." Edited by W. H. CREMER, of Regent Street. With nearly 200 Illustrations. Crown 8vo, cloth extra, price 4*s.* 6*d.*

Hatton's (Jos.)

Kites and Pigeons. A most amusing Novelette. With Illustrations by LINLEY SAMBOURNE, of "Punch." Fcap. 8vo, illustrated wrapper, 1*s.*

Hawthorne's

English and American Note Books. Edited, with an Introduction, by MONCURE D. CONWAY. Royal 16mo, paper cover, 1*s.*; in cloth, 1*s.* 6*d.*

Hall's (Mrs. S. C.) Sketches of Irish
Character. With numerous Illustrations on Steel and Wood, by
DANIEL MACLISE, R.A., Sir JOHN GILBERT, W. HARVEY, and
G. CRUIKSHANK. 8vo, pp. 450, cloth extra, 7s. 6d.

"'The Irish sketches of this lady resemble Miss Mitford's beautiful English
Sketches in 'Our Village,' but they are far more vigorous and picturesque and
bright."—*Blackwood's Magazine.*

Hans Breitmann's Ballads. By J. G.
LELAND. The Complete Work, from the Author's revised Edition.
Royal 16mo, paper cover, 1s.; in cloth, 1s. 6d.

Hollingshead's "Plain English." By
JOHN HOLLINGSHEAD, of the Gaiety Theatre. Crown 8vo, illustrated cover, 1s.   [*Preparing.*

Hone's Scrap-Books: The Miscellaneous

Writings of WILLIAM HONE, Author of "The Table-Book," "Every-Day Book," and the "Year Book:" being a supplementary volume to those works. Now first collected. With Notes, Portraits, and numerous Illustrations of curious and eccentric objects. Crown 8vo, cloth extra, 7*s.* 6*d.* [*Preparing.*

THE MOST COMPLETE HOGARTH EVER PUBLISHED.

THE TALKING HAND.

Hogarth's Works : with Life and Anecdotal

Descriptions of the Pictures, by JOHN IRELAND and JOHN NICHOLS. The Work includes 150 Engravings, reduced in exact facsimile of the Original Plates, specimens of which have now become very scarce. The whole in Three Series, 8vo, cloth, gilt, 22*s.* 6*d.* Each series is, however, Complete in itself, and is sold separately at 7*s.* 6*d.*

Hogarth's Five Days' Frolic; or, Pere-

grinations by Land and Water. Illustrated with Tinted Drawings, made by HOGARTH and SCOTT during the Journey. 4to, beautifully printed, cloth, extra gilt, 10*s.* 6*d.* ·

*** *A graphic and most extraordinary picture of the hearty English times in which these merry artists lived.*

---

74 & 75, *PICCADILLY, LONDON, W.*

OLIVER WENDELL HOLMES' WORKS.

Holmes' Autocrat of the Breakfast
Table. An entirely New Edition of this Favourite Work. Royal
16mo, paper cover, 1s.; in cloth, neat, 1s. 6d.

Holmes' Poet at the Breakfast Table.
From January to June. Paper cover, 1s.

Holmes' Professor at the Breakfast
Table. A Companion Volume to the "Autocrat of the Breakfast
Table." Royal 16mo, paper cover, 1s. ; cloth neat, 1s. 6d.

Holmes' Wit and Humour. Delightful
Verses, in the style of the elder Hood. Fcap. 8vo, illustrated
wrapper, 1s.

Hood's Whims and Odditties. The
Entire Work. Now issued Complete, the Two Parts in One Volume,
with all the Humorous Designs. Royal 16mo, paper cover, 1s. ; cloth
neat, 1s. 6d.

Hunt's (Leigh) Tale for a Chimney
Corner, and other charming Essays. With Introduction by EDMUND
OLLIER, and Portrait supplied by the late THORNTON HUNT.
Royal 16mo, paper cover, 1s. 4d. ; cloth neat, 1s. 10d.

Hunt's (Robert, F.R.S.) Drolls of Old
Cornwall; or, POPULAR ROMANCES OF THE WEST OF ENG-
LAND. New Edition, Complete in One Volume, with Illustra-
tions by GEORGE CRUIKSHANK. Crown 8vo, extra cloth gilt,
7s. 6d.
⁎ "Mr. Hunt's charming book on the Drolls and Stories of the West of
England."—*Saturday Review.*

Josh Billings: His Book of Sayings.
With Introduction by E. P. HINGSTON, Companion of Artemus
Ward when on his "Travels." Fcap. 8vo, illustrated cover, 1s.

Jennings' (Hargrave)
One of the Thirty. With curious Illustrations. Crown 8vo, cloth extra, 10s. 6d.

** An extraordinary narrative, tracing down one of the accursed pieces of silver for which Jesus of Nazareth was sold. Through eighteen centuries is this fated coin tracked, now in the possession of the innocent, now in the grasp of the guilty, but everywhere carrying with it the evil that fell upon Judas.

Jennings' (Hargrave)
The Rosicrucians: Their Rites and **Mysteries.** With Chapters on the Ancient Fire and Serpent Worshippers, and Explanations of the Mystic Symbols represented in the Monuments and Talismans of the Primeval Philosophers. Crown 8vo, cloth extra, with about 300 Illustrations, 10s 6d.

Jerrold's (Blanchard) Cent. per Cent.
A Story Written on a Bill Stamp. A New Edition. Fcap. 8vo, illustrated boards, 2s. [*Nearly ready.*

Jerrold's (Douglas) Brownrigg
Papers: The Actress at the Duke's; Baron von Boots; Christopher Snubb; The Tutor Fiend and his Three Pupils; Papers of a Gentleman at Arms, &c. By DOUGLAS JERROLD. Edited by his son, BLANCHARD JERROLD. Post 8vo. Illustrated boards, 2s. [*Nearly ready.*

Kalendars of Gwynedd. Compiled by
EDWARD BREESE, F.S.A. With Notes by WILLIAM WATKIN EDWARD WYNNE, Esq., F.S.A., of Penairth. Demy 4to, cloth extra, 28s. ❦

The Knowing Ones at Home. Stories
of their Doings at a Local Science Meeting, at the Crystal Palace, at St. Paul's, at a Foresters' Fête, &c., &c. A New and entirely Original Humorous Story, crammed with Fun from the first page to the last. Profusely Illustrated by BRUNTON, MATT MORGAN, and other Artists. Fcap. 4to, illustrated wrapper, price 1s.

Lamb's (Charles) Essays of Elia. The

Two SERIES, Complete in One Volume. Royal 16mo, uniform with "Leigh Hunt's Essays," paper cover, 1s.; cloth extra, 1s. 6d.

Lamb (Mary & Charles) : Their Poems,

Letters, and Remains. Now first collected, with Reminiscences and Notes, by W. CAREW HAZLITT. With HANCOCK'S Portrait of the Essayist, Facsimiles of the Title-pages of the rare First Editions of

ROSAMUND GRAY'S COTTAGE.

Lamb's and Coleridge's Works, Facsimile of a Page of the Original MS. of the "Essay on Roast Pig," and numerous Illustrations of Lamb's Favourite Haunts in London and the Suburbs. Crown 8vo, cloth extra, price 10s. 6d.; or, LARGE-PAPER COPIES (a limited number only printed), price 21s.

Life in London ; or,

The Day and Night Scenes of Jerry Hawthorn and Corinthian Tom. WITH THE WHOLE OF CRUIKSHANK'S VERY DROLL ILLUSTRATIONS, in Colours, after the Originals. Crown 8vo, cloth extra, 7s. 6d.

*** *One of the most popular books ever issued, and often quoted by Thackeray, who devotes one of his "Roundabout Papers" to a description of it.*

Literary Scraps. A Folio Scrap-Book of

340 columns, with guards, for the reception of Cuttings from News-papers, Extracts, Miscellanea, &c. A very useful book. In folio, half-roan, cloth sides, 7s. 6d.

Little Breeches, and other Pieces (PIKE

COUNTY BALLADS). By Colonel JOHN HAY. Foolscap 8vo, illustrated cover, 1s. 6d.

The Little London Directory of 1677.

The Oldest Printed List of the Merchants and Bankers of London. Reprinted from the Rare Original, with an Introduction by JOHN CAMDEN HOTTEN. 16mo, binding after the original, 6s. 6d.

Henry Wadsworth Longfellow's Prose

Works, Complete, including his Stories and Essays, "Outre-Mer," "Hyperion," "Kavanagh," "Drift-wood," "On the Poets and Poetry of Europe," now for the first time collected. Edited, with an Introduction, by the Author of "Tennyson-iana." With Portrait and Illustrations, drawn by VALENTINE W. BROMLEY. 800 pages, crown 8vo, cloth gilt, 7s. 6d.

** The reader will find the present edition of Longfellow's Prose Writings by far the most complete ever issued in this country. "Outre-Mer" contains two additional chapters, restored from the first edition; while "The Poets and Poetry of Europe," and the little collection of Sketches entitled "Driftwood," are now first introduced to the English public.

Lost Beauties of the English Language.

An Appeal to Authors, Poets, Clergymen, and Public Speakers. By CHARLES MACKAY, LL.D. Crown 8vo, cloth extra, 6s. 6d.

Madre Natura *versus* The

Moloch of Fashion. By LUKE LIM-NER. With 32 Illustrations by the Author. FOURTH EDITION, revised, corrected and enlarged. Crown 8vo, cloth extra gilt, red edges, price 2s. 6d.

"Agreeably written and amusingly illustrated. Common sense and erudition are brought to bear on the subjects discussed in it."—*Lancet.*

The Log of the Water Lily, during Three

Cruises on the Rhine, Neckar, Main, Moselle, Danube, Saone, and
Rhone.   By R. B. MANSFIELD, B.A.   Illustrated by ALFRED
THOMPSON, B.A.   Fifth Edition, revised and considerably Enlarged.
Crown 8vo, cloth extra, gilt, 5s.

COMPANION TO "THE SECRET OUT."

The Magician's Own Book.   Ample

Instructions for Performances with Cups and Balls, Eggs, Hats,
Handkerchiefs, &c.   All from Actual Experience.   Edited by W. H.
CREMER, of Regent Street.   Cloth extra, 200 Illustrations, 4s. 6d.

Magna Charta.   An exact Facsimile of the

Original Document, preserved in the British Museum, very carefully
drawn, and printed on fine plate paper, nearly 3 feet long by 2 feet
wide, with the Arms and Seals of the Barons elaborately emblazoned
in Gold and Colours.   A.D. 1215.   Price 5s.; or, handsomely framed
and glazed, in carved oak, of an antique pattern, 22s. 6d.

A full Translation, with Notes, has been prepared, price 6d.

ENTIRELY NEW GAMES.

The Merry Circle, and How the Visitors

were entertained during Twelve Pleasant Evenings.   A Book of
New Intellectual Games and Amusements.   Edited by Mrs. CLARA
BELLEW.   Crown 8vo, numerous Illustrations, cloth extra, 4s. 6d.

. *An excellent book to consult before going to an evening party.*

MARK TWAIN'S WORKS.
AUTHOR'S CORRECTED EDITION.

Mark Twain's Choice Works. Revised
and Corrected by the Author. With a Life, a Portrait of the Author, and numerous Illustrations. 700 pages, cloth gilt, 7*s*. 6*d*.

Mark Twain's Inno-
cents Abroad : The Voyage Out. Crown 8vo, cloth, fine toned paper, 3*s*. 6*d*.; or fcap. 8vo, illustrated wrapper, 1*s*.

Mark Twain's New
Pilgrim's Progress : The Voyage Home. Crown 8vo, cloth, fine toned paper, 3*s*. 6*d*. ; or fcap. 8vo, illustrated wrapper, 1*s*.|

Mark Twain's Bur-
lesque Autobiography, First Mediæval Romance, and on Children. Fcap. 8vo, illustrated cover, 6*d*.

Mark Twain's Eye-Openers. A Volume
of immensely Funny Sayings, and Stories that will bring a smile upon the gruffest countenance. Fcap. 8vo, illustrated wrapper, 1*s*.

Mark Twain's Jumping Frog, and other
Humorous Sketches. Fcap. 8vo, illustrated cover, 1*s*.
" An inimitably funny book."—*Saturday Review.*

Mark Twain's Pleasure Trip on the
Continent of Europe. (The "Innocents Abroad" and "New Pilgrim's Progress" in One Volume.) 500 pages, paper boards, 2*s*.; or in cloth, 2*s*. 6*d*.

Mark Twain's Practical Jokes ; or,
Mirth with Artemus Ward, and other Papers. By MARK TWAIN, and other Humorists. Fcap. 8vo, illustrated cover, 1*s*.

Mark Twain's Screamers. A Gathering
of Delicious Bits and Short Stories. Fcap. 8vo, illustrated cover, 1*s*.

Mayhew's London Characters : Illus-
trations of the Humour, Pathos, and Peculiarities of London Life.
By HENRY MAYHEW, Author of "London Labour and the London
Poor," and other Writers. With nearly 100 graphic Illustrations.
Crown 8vo, cloth gilt, about 500 pages, 6s.

Monumental Inscriptions of the West
Indies, from the Earliest Date, with Genealogical and Historical
Annotations, &c., from Original, Local, and other Sources. Illustrative of the Histories and Genealogies of the Seventeenth Century,
the Calendars of State Papers, Peerages, and Baronetages. With
Engravings of the Arms of the principal Families. Chiefly collected
on the spot by the Author, Capt. J. H. LAWRENCE-ARCHER. One
volume, demy 4to, about 300 pages, cloth extra, 21s.

Mr. Brown on the Goings-on of Mrs.
Brown at the Tichborne Trial, &c. Fcap. 8vo, illustrated cover, 1s.

Mr. Sprouts: His Opinions. Fcap. 8vo,
illustrated cover, 1s.

UNIFORM WITH "TOM D'URFEY'S PILLS."

Musarum Deliciæ; or, The Muses' Re-
creation, 1656; Wit Restor'd, 1658; and Wit's Recreations, 1640.
The whole compared with the originals ; with all the Wood Engravings, Plates, Memoirs, and Notes. A New Edition, in 2 volumes,
post 8vo, beautifully printed on antique laid paper, and bound in
antique boards, 21s. A few Large Paper copies have been prepared,
price 35s.

*⁎⁎ Of the Poets of the Restoration, there are none whose works are more rare
than those of Sir John Mennis and Dr. James Smith. The small volume entitled
"Musarum Deliciæ ; or, The Muses' Recreation," which contains the productions
of these two friends, was not accessible to Mr. Freeman when he compiled his
"Kentish Poets," and has since become so rare that it is only found in the cabinets
of the curious. A reprint of the "Musarum Deliciæ," together with several other
kindred pieces of the period, appeared in 1817, forming two volumes of Facetiæ,
edited by Mr. E. Dubois, author of "The Wreath," &c. These volumes having in
turn become exceedingly scarce, the Publishers venture to put forth the present new
edition, in which, while nothing has been omitted, no pains have been spared to
render it more complete and elegant than any that has yet appeared. The type,
plates, and woodcuts of the originals have been accurately followed ; the notes of
the Editor of 1817 are considerably augmented, and indexes have been added,
together with a portrait of Sir John Mennis, from a painting by Vandyke in Lord
Clarendon's Collection.*

The Mystery of Mr. E. Drood. An

Adaptation. By ORPHEUS C. KERR. Fcap. 8vo, illustrated cover, 1s.

The Mystery of the Good Old Cause:

Sarcastic Notices of those Members of the Long Parliament that held Places, both Civil and Military, contrary to the Self-denying Ordinance of April 3, 1645; with the Sums of Money and Lands they divided among themselves. Small 4to, half-morocco, 7s. 6d.

Never Caught in Blockade-Running.

An exciting book of Adventures during the American Civil War. Fcap. 8vo, illustrated cover, 1s.

Nuggets and Dust, panned out in Cali-

fornia by DOD GRILE. Selected and edited by J. MILTON SLOLUCK. A new style of Humour and Satire. Fcap. 8vo, illustrated cover, 1s.

. *If Artemus Ward may be considered the Douglas Jerrold, and Mark Twain the Sydney Smith of America, Dod Grile will rank as their Dean Swift.*

ARTHUR O'SHAUGHNESSY'S POEMS.

Music and Moonlight: Poems and Songs.

By ARTHUR O'SHAUGHNESSY, Author of "An Epic of Women." Fcap. 8vo, cloth extra, 7s. 6d.

An Epic of Women, and other Poems.

By ARTHUR O'SHAUGHNESSY. Illustrated by J. T. NETTLESHIP. SECOND EDITION. Fcap. 8vo, cloth extra, 6s.

"Of the formal art of poetry he is in many senses quite a master; his metres are not only good,—they are his own, and often of an invention most felicitous as well as careful."—*Academy.*

"With its quaint title and quaint illustrations, 'An Epic of Women' will be a rich treat to a wide circle of admirers."—*Athenæum.*

"Many of his verses are exceedingly beautiful; like a delicious melody."—*Examiner.*

The Old Prose Stories whence TENNYSON'S

"Idylls of the King" were taken. By B. M. RANKING. Royal 16mo, paper cover, 1s.; cloth extra, 1s. 6d.

Napoleon III., the Man of His Time;

from Caricatures. PART I. THE STORY OF THE LIFE OF NAPOLEON III., as told by J. M. HASWELL.

PART II. THE SAME STORY, as told by the POPULAR CARICATURES of the past Thirty-five Years. Crown 8vo, with Coloured Frontispiece and over 100 Caricatures, 400 pp., 7s. 6d.

⁎ *The object of this Work is to give Both Sides of the Story. The Artist has gone over the entire ground of Continental and English Caricatures for the last third of a century, and a very interesting book is the result.*

Original Lists of Persons of Quality;

Emigrants; Religious Exiles; Political Rebels; Serving Men Sold for a Term of Years; Apprentices; Children Stolen; Maidens Pressed; and others who went from Great Britain to the American Plantations, 1600–1700. With their Ages, the Localities where they formerly Lived in the Mother Country, Names of the Ships in which they embarked, and other interesting particulars. From MSS. preserved in the State Paper Department of Her Majesty's Public Record Office, England. Edited by JOHN CAMDEN HOTTEN. A very handsome volume, crown 4to, cloth gilt, 700 pages, 31s. 6d. A few Large Paper copies have been printed, price 50s.

74 & 75, *PICCADILLY, LONDON, W.*

THE OLD DRAMATISTS.

Ben Jonson's Works. With Notes, Critical and Explanatory, and a Biographical Memoir by WILLIAM GIFFORD. Edited by Lieut.-Col. FRANCIS CUNNINGHAM. Complete in 3 vols., crown 8vo, Portrait. Cloth, 6s. each; cloth gilt, 6s. 6d. each.

George Chapman's Plays, Complete, from the Original Quartos. With an Introduction by ALGERNON CHARLES SWINBURNE. Crown 8vo, Portrait. Cloth, 6s.; cloth gilt, 6s. 6d.

[Nearly ready.

Christopher Marlowe's Works: Including his Translations. Edited, with Notes and Introduction, by Lieut.-Col. F. CUNNINGHAM. Crown 8vo, Portrait. Cloth, 6s.; cloth gilt, 6s. 6d.

Philip Massinger's Plays. From the Text of WM. GIFFORD. With the addition of the Tragedy of "Believe as You List." Edited by Lieut.-Col. FRANCIS CUNNINGHAM. Crown 8vo, Portrait. Cloth, 6s.; cloth gilt, 6s. 6d.

Parochial History of the County of Cornwall. Compiled from the best authorities, and corrected and improved from actual survey. 4 vols. 4to, cloth extra, £3 3s. the set; or, separately, the first three volumes, 16s. each; the fourth volume, 18s.

COMPANION TO "CUSSANS' HERALDRY."

The Pursuivant of Arms;
or, Heraldry founded upon Facts. A Popular Guide to the Science of Heraldry. By J. R. PLANCHÉ, Esq., F.S.A., Somerset Herald. To which are added, Essays on the BADGES OF THE HOUSES OF LANCASTER AND YORK. A New Edition, enlarged and revised by the Author, illustrated with Coloured Frontispiece, five full-page Plates, and about 200 Illustrations. Crown 8vo, beautifully bound in cloth, with Emblematic Design, extra gilt, 7s. 6d.

SEVENTH EDITION OF

Puck on Pegasus.

By H. CHOLMONDELEY-PENNELL. Profusely illustrated by the late JOHN LEECH, H. K. BROWNE, Sir NOEL PATON, JOHN MILLAIS, JOHN TENNIEL, RICHARD DOYLE, Miss ELLEN EDWARDS, and other artists. A New Edition (the SEVENTH), crown 8vo, cloth extra, gilt, price 5s.; or gilt edges, 6s.

*** *This most amusing work has received everywhere the highest praise as "a clever and brilliant book."*

" The book is clever and amusing, vigorous and healthy."—*Saturday Review.*

"The epigrammatic drollery of Mr. Cholmondeley-Pennell's ' Puck on Pegasus' is well known to many of our readers. . . . The present *(the sixth)* is a superb and handsomely printed and illustrated edition of the book."—*Times.*

"Specially fit for reading in the family circle."—*Observer.*

By the same Author.

Modern Babylon, and other Poems.

Small crown 8vo, cloth extra, gilt, 4s. 6d.

Policeman Y: His Opinions on War

and the Millingtary. With Illustrations by the Author, JOHN EDWARD SODEN. Cloth, very neat, 2s. 6d. ; in paper, 1s.

IMPORTANT TO ALL INTERESTED IN MINES.

The Practical Assayer: A Guide to

Miners and Explorers. By OLIVER NORTH, of "The Field," "Mining Journal," &c. With numerous Tables and Illustrative Woodcuts. Crown 8vo, cloth extra, 7s. 6d.

*** *This book gives directions, in the plainest and simplest form, for assaying bullion and the baser metals by the cheapest, quickest, and best methods. Persons interested in mining property will be enabled, by following the instructions given, to form a tolerably correct idea of the value of ores, without any previous knowledge of assaying ; while to the young man intending to seek his fortune abroad in mining countries it is indispensable.*

74 & 75, *PICCADILLY, LONDON, W.*

"AN AWFULLY JOLLY BOOK FOR PARTIES."

Puniana: Thoughts

Wise and Otherwise. By the Hon. HUGH ROWLEY. Best Book of Riddles and Puns ever formed. With nearly 100 exquisitely Fanciful Drawings. Contains nearly 3000 of the best Riddles, and 10,000 most outrageous Puns, and is one of the most Popular Books ever issued. New Edition, small quarto, uniform with the " Bab Ballads." Price 6s.

"Enormous burlesque — unapproachable and pre-eminent. We think this very queer volume will be a favourite. We should suggest that, to a dull person desirous to get credit with the young holiday people, it would be good policy to invest in the book and dole it out by instalments."—*Saturday Review.*

By the same Author.

A Second Series of Puniana: Containing

nearly 100 beautifully executed Drawings, and a splendid Collection of Riddles and Puns, fully equal to those in the First Volume. Small 4to, uniform with the First Series, cl. gt., gt. edges, 6s.[*Preparing.*

Private Book of Useful Alloys and

Memoranda for Goldsmiths and Jewellers. By JAMES E. COLLINS, C.E. Royal 16mo, 3s. 6d. *Invaluable to the Trade.*

UNIFORM WITH "WONDERFUL CHARACTERS."

Remarkable Trials and Notorious

Characters. From "Half-Hanged Smith," 1700, to Oxford, who shot at the Queen, 1840. By Captain L. BENSON. With spirited full-page Engravings by PHIZ. 8vo, 550 pages, 7s. 6d.

** *A Complete Library of Sensation Literature! There are plots enough here to produce a hundred "exciting" Novels, and at least five hundred "powerful" Magazine Stories. The book will be appreciated by all readers whose taste lies in this direction.*

UNIFORM WITH "THE TURF, CHASE, AND ROAD."

Reminiscences of the late Thomas

Assheton Smith, Esq.; or, The Pursuits of an English Country Gentleman. By Sir J. E. EARDLEY WILMOT, Bart. A New and Revised Edition, with Steel-plate Portrait, and plain and coloured Illustrations. Crown 8vo, cloth extra, 7s. 6d.

GUSTAVE DORÉ'S DESIGNS.

The Works of Rabelais.   Faithfully trans-
lated from the French, with variorum Notes, and numerous characteristic Illustrations by GUSTAVE DORÉ.   Crown 8vo, cloth extra,
700 pages.   Price 7s. 6d.

Roll of Battle Abbey; or, A List of the Prin-
cipal Warriors who came over from Normandy with William the
Conqueror, and Settled in this Country, A.D. 1066-7.   Carefully
drawn, and printed on fine plate paper, nearly three feet by two
feet, with the Arms of the principal Barons elaborately emblazoned
in Gold and Colours.   Price 5s. ; or, handsomely framed in carved
oak of an antique pattern, 22s. 6d.

Roll of Caerlaverock: the Oldest Heraldic
Roll; including the Original Anglo-Norman Poem, and an English
Translation of the MS. in the British Museum.   By THOMAS
WRIGHT, M.A.   The Arms emblazoned in gold and colours.   In
4to, very handsomely printed, extra gold cloth, 12s.

Rochefoucauld's Reflections and

Moral Maxims. With Introductory Essay by SAINTE-BEUVE, and Explanatory Notes. Royal 16mo, elegantly printed, 1s. ; cloth neat, 1s. 6d.

Roman Catholics in the County of

York in 1604. Transcribed from the Original MS. in the Bodleian Library, and Edited, with Genealogical Notes, by EDWARD PEACOCK, F.S.A., Editor of "Army Lists of the Roundheads and Cavaliers, 1642." Small 4to, handsomely printed and bound, 15s.

** Genealogists and Antiquaries will find much new and curious matter in this work. An elaborate Index refers to every name in the volume, among which will be found many of the highest local interest.

Ross's (Chas. H.) Unlikely Tales and

Wrong-Headed Essays. Fcap. 8vo, with numerous quaint and amusing Illustrations, 1s.

Ross's (Chas. H.) Story of a Honey-

moon. A New Edition of this charmingly humorous book, with numerous Illustrations by the Author. Fcap. 8vo, picture boards, 2s.

School Life at Winchester College;

or, The Reminiscences of a Winchester Junior. By the Author of "The Log of the Water Lily;" and "The Water Lily on the Danube." Second Edition, Revised, COLOURED PLATES, 7s. 6d.

Shaving Them; or, The Adventures of

Three Yankees. By TITUS A. BRICK. Fcap. 8vo, illustrated cover, 1s.

THE RUMP PARLIAMENT.

The Rump; or, An Exact Collection of

the choicest POEMS and SONGS relating to the late Times, and
continued by the most eminent Wits; from Anno 1639 to 1661. A
Facsimile Reprint of the rare Original Edition (London, 1662), with
Frontispiece and Engraved Title-page. In 2 vols., large fcap. 8vo,
printed on antique laid paper, made expressly for the work, and bound
in antique boards, 17s. 6d. ; or, LARGE-PAPER COPIES, 30s.

[Nearly ready.

*** *A very rare and extraordinary collection of some two hundred Popular
Ballads and Cavalier Songs, on all the principal incidents of the great Civil War,
the Trial of Strafford, the Martyrdom of King Charles, the Commonwealth,
Cromwell, Pym, the Roundheads, &c. It was from such materials that Lord
Macaulay was enabled to produce his vivid pictures of England in the sixteenth
century. To historical students and antiquaries, and to the general reader, these
volumes will be found full of interest.*

The Secret

Out; or, One Thousand
Tricks with Cards, and
other Recreations; with
Entertaining Experiments
in Drawing Room or
" White Magic." By the
Author of the " Magi-
cian's Own Book." Edited
by W. H. CREMER, Jun.,
of Regent Street. With
300 Engravings. Crown
8vo, cloth, 4s. 6d.

*** *Under the title of "Le Ma-
gicien des Salons," this book has
long been a Standard Magic Book with all French and German Professors of the
Art.*

Sheridan's (Richard Brinsley) Com-

plete Works, with Life and Anecdotes. Including his Dramatic
Writings, printed from the Original Editions, his works in Prose
and Poetry, Translations, Speeches, Jokes, Puns, &c.; with a Collection of Sheridaniana. Crown 8vo, cloth gilt, with Portraits and
Illustrations, 7s. 6d.

Shirley Brooks' Amusing Poetry. A

Selection of Humorous Verse from all the Best Writers. Edited, with
a Preface, by SHIRLEY BROOKS, Editor of *Punch.* A New Edition,
in fcap. 8vo, cloth extra, gilt, and gilt edges, 3s. 6d.

Shelley's Early Life. From Original

Sources. With Curious Incidents, Letters, and Writings, now
First Published or Collected, By DENIS FLORENCE MAC-CARTHY.
Cheaper Edition, crown 8vo, with Illustrations, 440 pages, 7s. 6d.

*** *The poet's political pamphlets, advocating Home Rule and other rights,
are here for the first time given in a collected form.*

THE POCKET SHELLEY.

SHELLEY, FROM THE GODWIN SKETCH.

Shelley's Poetical Works. Now First

Reprinted from the Author's Original Editions. In Two Series, the
FIRST containing "Queen Mab" and the Early Poems; the SECOND,
"Laon and Cythna," "The Cenci," and Later Poems. In royal
16mo, thick volumes. Price of the FIRST SERIES, 1s. 8d. illustrated
cover, 2s. 2d. cloth extra; SECOND SERIES, 1s. 8d. illustrated cover,
2s. 2d. cloth extra.

The Third Series, completing the Work, will shortly be ready.

CHARLES DICKENS' EARLY SKETCHES.

Sketches of Young Couples, Young

Ladies and Young Gentlemen. By "QUIZ" (CHARLES DICKENS).
With 18 Steel-plate Illustrations by "PHIZ" (H. K. BROWNE).
Crown 8vo, cloth gilt, 4s. 6d.

74 & 75, PICCADILLY, LONDON, W.

Signboards: Their History. With Anecdotes of Famous Taverns and Remarkable Characters. By JACOB LARWOOD and JOHN CAMDEN HOTTEN. SEVENTH EDITION. Crown 8vo, cloth extra, 580 pp., 7s. 6d.

HELP ME THROUGH THIS WORLD !

"It is not fair on the part of a reviewer to pick out the plums of an author's book, thus filching away his cream, and leaving little but skim-milk remaining; but, even if we were ever so maliciously inclined, we could not in the present instance pick out all Messrs. Larwood and Hotten's plums, because the good things are so numerous as to defy the most wholesale depredation."—*The Times.*

** *Nearly 100 most curious illustrations on wood are given, showing the various old signs which were formerly hung from taverns and other houses.*

The Slang Dictionary: Etymological, Historical, and Anecdotal. An ENTIRELY NEW EDITION, revised throughout, and considerably Enlarged, containing upwards of a thousand more words than the last edition. Crown 8vo, with Curious Illustrations, cloth extra, 6s. 6d.

"Valuable as a work of reference."—*Saturday Review.*

A KEEPSAKE FOR SMOKERS.

The Smoker's Text-Book. By J. HAMER, F.R.S.L. Exquisitely printed from "silver-faced" type, cloth, very neat, gilt edges, 2s. 6d., post free.

WEST-END LIFE AND DOINGS.

The Story of the London Parks. By

JACOB LARWOOD. With numerous Illustrations, Coloured and Plain. In One thick Volume, crown 8vo, cloth extra, gilt, 7s. 6d.

** A most interesting work, giving a complete History of these favourite out-of-door resorts, from the earliest period to the present time.

CHARMING NEW TRAVEL-BOOK.

"It may be we shall touch the happy isles."

Summer Cruising in the South Seas.

By CHARLES WARREN STODDARD. With nearly Thirty Engravings on Wood, drawn by WALLIS MACKAY. Crown 8vo, cloth, extra gilt, 7s. 6d.

** Chapters descriptive of life and adventure in the South Sea Islands, in the style made so popular by " The Earl and the Doctor."

"A remarkable book, which has a certain wild picturesqueness."—*Standard.*

"The author's experiences are very amusingly related, and, in parts, with much freshness and originality."—*Judy.*

"Mr. Stoddard is a humourist; 'Summer Cruising' has a good deal of undeniable amusement."—*Nation.*

74 & 75, PICCADILLY, LONDON, W.

ALGERNON CHARLES SWINBURNE'S WORKS.

Swinburne's Atalanta in Calydon.
New Edition.   Foolscap 8vo, price 6s.

Swinburne's Bothwell.   A New Poem.
[*In preparation.*

Swinburne's Chastelard.   A Tragedy,
New Edition.   Price 7s.

Swinburne's Poems and Ballads.
New Edition.   Price 9s.

Swinburne's Notes on his Poems,
and on the Reviews which have appeared upon them.   Price 1s.

Swinburne's Queen Mother and Rosa-
mond.   New Edition.   Foolscap 8vo, price 5s.

Swinburne's Song of Italy.   Foolscap
8vo, toned paper, cloth, price 3s. 6d.

Swinburne's William Blake: A Critical
Essay.   With facsimile Paintings, Coloured by Hand, after the Drawings by Blake and his Wife.   Thick 8vo, cloth extra, price 16s.

WILLIAM COMBE'S BEST WORK.

Dr. Syntax's Three Tours. WITH THE
WHOLE OF ROWLANDSON'S VERY DROLL FULL-PAGE ILLUSTRA-
TIONS, IN COLOURS, AFTER THE ORIGINAL DRAWINGS. Com-
prising the well-known TOURS—

> 1. IN SEARCH OF THE PICTURESQUE.
> 2. IN SEARCH OF CONSOLATION.
> 3. IN SEARCH OF A WIFE.

The Three Series Complete and Unabridged, with a Life of the
Author by JOHN CAMDEN HOTTEN. 8vo, cloth extra, gilt, in one
handsome volume, price 7*s.* 6*d.*

** *One of the most amusing and laughable books ever published.*

A SMALLER EDITION, with Eight Coloured Plates, the text complete,
price 3*s.* 6*d.*

Taylor's History of Playing Cards.
With Sixty curious Illustrations, 550 pp., price 7*s.* 6*d.*

** *Ancient and Modern Games, Conjuring, Fortune-Telling, and Card Sharp-*
ing, Gambling and Calculation, Cartomancy, Old Gaming-Houses, Card Revels
and Blind Hookey, Picquet and Vingt-et-un, Whist and Cribbage, Tricks, &c.

Theseus: A Greek Fairy Legend.
Illustrated, in a series of Designs in Gold and Sepia, by JOHN MOYR
SMITH. With descriptive text. Oblong folio, price 7*s.* 6*d.*

Thackerayana. Notes

and Anecdotes illustrative of Scenes and Characters in the Works of WILLIAM MAKEPEACE THACKERAY. With nearly Four Hundred Illustrations, coloured and plain. In 8vo, uniform with the Library Edition of his works, 7s. 6d. [*Nearly ready.*

Theodore Hook's

Choice Humorous Works, with his Ludicrous Adventures, Bons-mots, Puns, and Hoaxes. With a new Life of the Author, PORTRAITS, FACSIMILES, and ILLUSTRATIONS. Cr. 8vo, 600 pages, cloth extra, 7s. 6d.

*** "As a wit and humourist of the highest order his name will be preserved. His political songs and *jeux d'esprit*, when the hour comes for collecting them, *will form a volume of sterling and lasting attraction!*"—J. G. LOCKHART.

Theodore Hook's Ramsbottom

Papers. Twenty-nine Letters, complete. Fcap. 8vo, illust. cover, 1s.

74 & 75, PICCADILLY, LONDON, W.

THE SUBSCRIPTION ROOM AT BROOKES'S.

Timbs' Clubs and Club Life in Lon-

don. With ANECDOTES of its FAMOUS COFFEE HOUSES, HOSTEL-
RIES, and TAVERNS. By JOHN TIMBS, F.S.A. New Edition,
with NUMEROUS ILLUSTRATIONS, drawn expressly. Crown 8vo,
cloth extra, 600 pages, 7s. 6d. ·

*** *A Companion to " The History of Sign-Boards."* *It abounds in quaint*
stories of the Blue Stocking, Kit-Kat, Beef Steak, Robin Hood, Mohocks, Scriblerus,
One o'Clock, the Civil, *and hundreds of other Clubs; together with* Tom's, Dick's,
Button's, Ned's, Will's, *and the famous Coffee Houses of the last century.*

Timbs' English Eccentrics and Ec-

centricities. Stories of Wealth and Fashion, Delusions, Impos-
tures and Fanatic Missions, Strange Sights and Sporting Scenes,
Eccentric Artists, Theatrical Folks, Men of Letters, &c. By JOHN
TIMBS, F.S.A. An entirely New Edition, with numerous Illustrations. Crown 8vo, cloth extra, 600 pages, 7s. 6d. [*Nearly ready.*

Victor Hugo's Les Misérables: Fantine.

, Now first published in an English Translation, complete and unabridged, with the exception of a few advisable omissions.   Post 8vo, illustrated boards, 2s.

"This work has somethimg more than the beauties of an exquisite style or the word-compelling power of a literary Zeus to recommend it to the tender care of a distant posterity : in dealing with all the emotions, passions, doubts, fears, which go to make up our common humanity, M. Victor Hugo has stamped upon every page the Hall-mark of genius and the loving patience and conscientious labour of a true artist. But the merits of 'Les Misérables' do not merely consist in the conception of it as a whole ; it abounds, page after page, with details of unequalled beauty."— *Quarterly Review.*

The next volume, COSETTE AND MARIUS, is nearly ready.

Vyner's Notitia Venatica: A Treatise

on Fox-Hunting, the General Management of Hounds, and the Diseases of Dogs; Distemper and Rabies; Kennel Lameness, &c. Sixth Edition, Enlarged. By ROBERT C. VYNER. WITH SPIRITED ILLUSTRATIONS IN COLOURS, BY ALKEN, OF MEMORABLE FOX-HUNTING SCENES.   Royal 8vo, cloth extra, 21s.

⁎⁎ *An entirely new edition of the best work on Fox-Hunting.*

Walt Whitman's Leaves of Grass.

The Complete Work, precisely as issued by the Author in Washington.   A thick volume, 8vo, green cloth, price 9s.

"Whitman is a poet who bears and needs to be read as a whole, and then the volume and torrent of his power carry the disfigurements along with it and away. He is really a fine fellow."—*Chambers's Journal.*

Warrant to Execute Charles I.   An

exact Facsimile of this important Document, with the Fifty-nine Signatures of the Regicides, and corresponding Seals, admirably executed on paper made to imitate the original document, 22 in. by 14 in.   Price 2s. ; or, handsomely framed and glazed in carved oak of antique pattern, 14s. 6d.

Warrant to Execute Mary Queen of

Scots.   The Exact Facsimile of this important Document, including the Signature of Queen Elizabeth and Facsimile of the Great Seal, on tinted paper, made to imitate the Original MS.   Price 2s.; or, handsomely framed and glazed in carved oak of antique pattern, 14s. 6d.

THE WATERFORD ROLL.
Illuminated Charter-Roll of Waterford, Temp. Richard II.

⁂ Amongst the Corporation Muniments of the City of Waterford is preserved an ancient Illuminated Roll, of great interest and beauty, comprising all the early Charters and Grants to the City of Waterford, from the time of Henry II. to Richard II. A full-length Portrait of each King, whose Charter is given—including Edward III., when young, and again at an advanced age—adorns the margin. These Portraits, with the exception of four which are smaller, and on one sheet of vellum, vary from eight to nine inches in length—some in armour, and some in robes of state. In addition to these are Portraits of an Archbishop in full canonicals, of a Chancellor, and of many of the chief Burgesses of the City of Waterford, as well as singularly curious Portraits of the Mayors of Dublin, Waterford, Limerick, and Cork, figured for the most part in the quaint bipartite costume of the Second Richard's reign, though partaking of many of the peculiarities of that of Edward III. Altogether this ancient work of art is unique of its kind in Ireland, and deserves to be rescued from oblivion, by the publication of the unedited Charters, and of fac-similes of all the Illuminations. The production of such a work would throw much light on the question of the art and social habits of the Anglo-Norman settlers in Ireland at the close of the fourteenth century. The Charters are, many of them, highly important from an historic point of view.

The Illuminations have been accurately traced and coloured for the work from a copy carefully made, by permission of the Mayor and Corporation of Waterford, by the late George V. Du Noyer, Esq., M.R.I.A.; and those Charters which have not already appeared in print will be edited by the Rev. James Graves, A.B., M.R.I.A., Hon. Sec. Kilkenny and South-East of Ireland Archæological Society.

The work will be brought out in the best manner, with embossed cover and characteristic title-page; and it will be put to press as soon as 250 subscribers are obtained. The price, in imperial 4to, is 20s. to subscribers, or 30s. to non-subscribers.

Wonderful Characters : Memoirs and Anecdotes of Remarkable and Eccentric Persons of Every Age and Nation. From the text of HENRY WILSON and JAMES CAULFIELD. Crown 8vo, cloth extra, with Sixty-one full-page Engravings of Extraordinary Persons, 7s. 6d.

⁂ There are so many curious matters discussed in this volume, that any person who takes it up will not readily lay it down until he has read it through. The Introduction is almost entirely devoted to a consideration of Pig-Faced Ladies, and the various stories concerning them.

Wright's (Andrew) Court-Hand Restored; or, Student's Assistant in Reading Old Deeds, Charters, Records, &c. Half Morocco, a New Edition, 10s. 6d.

⁂ The best guide to the reading of old Records, &c.

Wright's History of Caricature and the Grotesque in Art, in Literature, Sculpture, and Painting, from the Earliest Times to the Present Day. By THOMAS WRIGHT, Esq., M.A., F.S.A. Profusely illustrated by FAIRHOLT. Small 4to, cloth, extra gilt, red edges, 21s.

Wright's Caricature History of the

Georges (House of Hanover). A very entertaining Book of 640 pages, with 400 Pictures, Caricatures, Squibs, Broadsides, Window Pictures, &c. By THOMAS WRIGHT, Esq., M.A., F.S A. Crown 8vo, cloth extra, 7*s.* 6*d.*

" A set of caricatures such as we have in Mr. Wright's volume brings the surface of the age before us with a vividness that no prose writer, even of the highest power, could emulate. Macaulay's most brilliant sentence is weak by the side of the little woodcut from Gillray, which gives us Burke and Fox."—*Saturday Review.*

ALL THE BEST AMERICAN HUMOUR.

Yankee Drolleries. Edited by GEORGE

AUGUSTUS SALA. Containing ARTEMUS WARD, HIS BOOK ; BIGLOW PAPERS ; ORPHEUS C. KERR ; MAJOR JACK DOWNING ; and NASBY PAPERS. 700 pages, cloth, 3*s.* 6*d.*

More Yankee Drolleries. A Second

Series of the best American Humourists. Containing ARTEMUS WARD'S TRAVELS ; HANS BREITMANN ; THE PROFESSOR AT THE BREAKFAST TABLE ; BIGLOW PAPERS, Part II. ; and JOSH BILLINGS ; with an Introduction by GEORGE AUGUSTUS SALA. 700 pages, cloth, 3*s.* 6*d.*

A Third Supply of Yankee Drolleries.

Containing ARTEMUS WARD'S FENIANS ; THE AUTOCRAT OF THE BREAKFAST TABLE ; BRET HARTE'S STORIES ; THE INNOCENTS ABROAD ; and NEW PILGRIM'S PROGRESS ; with an Introduction by GEORGE AUGUSTUS SALA. 700 pages, cloth, 3*s.* 6*d.*

74 & 75, PICCADILLY, LONDON, W.